WALKING THE
EAST SUSSEX COAST

• A COMPANION GUIDE •

PHIL CHRISTIAN

Published in 2023
Copyright © 2023 Phil Christian

All rights reserved. Apart from any fair dealing for the purpose of private study, research, criticism or review, as permitted under the Copyright, Designs and Patents Act, 1988, no part of this publication may be reproduced, stored in a retrieval system, or transmitted in any form or by any means, electronic, electrical, chemical, mechanical, optical, photocopying, recording or otherwise, without the prior written permission of the copyright owner. Enquiries should be addressed to the Publishers.

Every attempt has been made by the author and publisher to secure the appropriate permissions for materials reproduced in this book. If there has been any oversight we will be happy to rectify the situation in future editions following a written submission made to the Publishers.

A CIP catalogue record for this book is available from the British Library.

ISBN: 978 0 85710 133 4

PiXZ Books
Halsgrove House, Ryelands Business Park,
Bagley Road, Wellington,
Somerset TA21 9PZ
Tel: 01823 653777
Fax: 01823 216796
email: sales@halsgrove.com

An imprint of Halstar Ltd, part of the Halsgrove group of companies.
Information on all Halsgrove titles is available at: www.halsgrove.com

Printed and bound in India by Parksons Graphics

Front cover: The Seven Sisters from Birling Gap.
Contents: Coastguard Cottages and the Seven Sisters.

CONTENTS

		Page
	Map	4
	Introduction	5
Chapter 1	HOVE, BRIGHTON, ROTTINGDEAN & SALTDEAN (PT 2)	7
Chapter 2	TELSCOMBE & PEACEHAVEN	24
Chapter 3	NEWHAVEN & PIDDINGHOE	30
Chapter 4	TIDE MILLS & SEAFORD	44
Chapter 5	LITLINGTON & WILMINGTON	53
Chapter 6	EXCEAT, CUCKMERE HAVEN & THE SEVEN SISTERS	62
Chapter 7	EAST DEAN, BIRLING GAP & BEACHY HEAD	70
Chapter 8	EASTBOURNE	79
Chapter 9	HERSTMONCEUX	90
Chapter 10	PEVENSEY & PEVENSEY BAY	97
Chapter 11	NORMANS BAY & BEXHILL	103
Chapter 12	BODIAM	112
Chapter 13	ST LEONARDS-ON-SEA & HASTINGS	118
Chapter 14	FAIRLIGHT, PETT & WINCHELSEA	129
Chapter 15	RYE & CAMBER	141
	Index	160

MAP OF COASTLINE AND WALK LOCATIONS

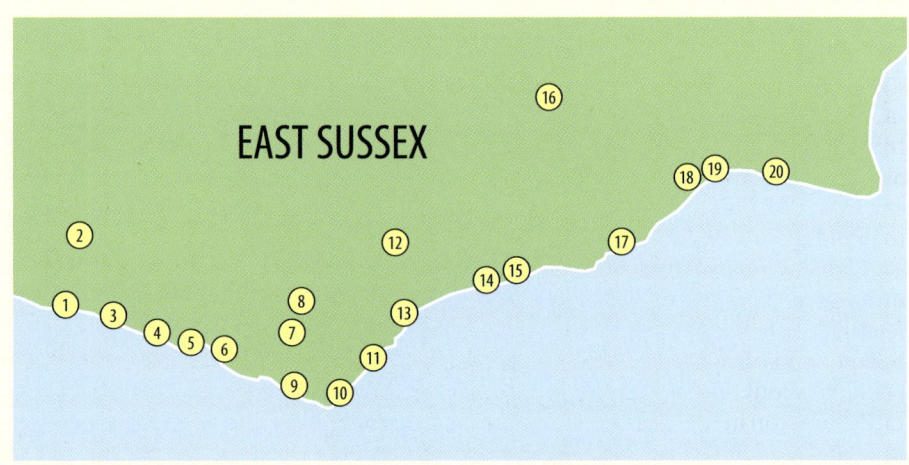

WALK	LOCATION	DISTANCE	ATTRACTION
1	Brighton	6.00mi 9.7km	Volks Electric Railway, Marina & Brighton Pavilion.
2	Brighton	2.25mi 3.6km	Chattri War Memorial.
3	Rottingdean & Saltdean	5.25mi 8.4km	Rottingdean Windmill, Roedean School & Undercliff.
4	Telscombe & Peacehaven	6.00mi 9.7km	Telscombe village church & Meridian Marker.
5	Newhaven & Piddinghoe	8.75mi 14.1km	Newhaven Fort, River Ouse and Piddinghoe Church.
6	Seaford	10.25mi 16.5km	Tide Mill ruins, Martello Tower (No.74), Seaford Head & Coastguard Cottages to Seven Sisters.
7	Litlington	3.75mi 6.0km	Litlington White Horse & Friston Forest.
8	Wilmington	2.25mi 3.6km	Long Man, Wilmington Madonna & 1600-year-old yew tree.
9	Exceat & Seven Sisters	8.75mi 14.1km	River Cuckmere, Seven Sisters & Exceat memorial stone.
10	East Dean & Beachy Head	8.25mi 13.3km	Sherlock Holmes' cottage, Birling Gap, 2 lighthouses & Beachy Head.
11	Eastbourne	11mi 17.7km	Pier, 3 x Martello Towers (No's 73, 66 & 64), Fort Redoubt & Sovereign Harbour.
12	Herstmonceux	3.25mi 5.2km	Herstmonceux Observatory & Castle.
13	Pevensey	4.5mi 7.2km	Castle, Court House Museum, 3 x Martello Towers (No's 60, 61 & 62) & Pevensey Levels / Bay.
14	Normans Bay	4.75mi 7.6km	Norman's Bay, Martello Tower (No. 55) & Star Inn.
15	Bexhill	3.25mi 5.2km	De La Warr Pavilion, Sackville Hotel, Manor House ruins, clock tower & Egerton Park.
16	Bodiam	5.75mi 9.3km	Bodiam Castle (Kent and Sussex Railway).
17	Hastings Country Park	4.5mi 7.2km	Hastings Country Park & Fairlight Radar Tower.
18	Winchelsea	3.5mi 5.6km	Historic Winchelsea, Spike Milligan's Grave and Royal Military Canal.
19	Rye Nature Reserve	8.0mi 12.9km	Rye Nature Reserve, Camber Castle & 2 x Martello Towers (No's 28 & 30).
20	Camber Sands	3.75mi 6.0km	Camber Sands beach and sand dunes.

INTRODUCTION

The Sussex coastline is about 90 miles (145 km) from Camber in East Sussex to the Chichester Harbour Area of Outstanding Natural Beauty in West Sussex. Including Brighton and Hove which is an independent borough and which is also included in my *West Sussex Companion Guide*, published in 2021, it is fair to say that East Sussex has about 50 miles (80 km) of coastline that is waiting for you to explore.

Unlike West Sussex the East Sussex coastline is one that you might want to walk in its entirety from Brighton to Camber as it offers a variety of stunning coastal features including dramatic cliffs, river estuaries, busy town seafronts, Levels, beaches and of course the famous sands at Camber. But that is not really what this book is about. I have walked the coastline from Hastings in East Sussex to Littlehampton in West Sussex in stages over a period of time and although enjoyable, logistically it was hampered by having to rely on public transport or needing a car at either end of the section you intend to walk. Also, if you want to do that you don't need a book, just walk with the sea beside you all the way.

This book is intended to help you appreciate local towns and villages and their relationship to the coast either historically or today. All the coastal towns and villages are featured and circular walks devised to walk as much of the coastline and visit as many places of interest as possible to help bring the area to life and to give you an understanding of where you are walking and its significance over time. A few inland walks have also been included for their relevance to the coast or for general interest. The East Sussex coast is also historically important for its coastal defences built to protect the south from attacks from Napoleon's army or from the Germans in WWII. Ten Martello Towers are described and visited on the walks as well as Newhaven Fort, Redoubt Fort in Eastbourne and Pevensey, Camber and Bodiam Castles. Throughout the coastal walks you are always close to the sea which is the English Channel and there is a section in the book giving you some information about the busiest shipping area in the world.

Martello Tower No.73, Eastbourne.

Undercliff path in high winds, Peacehaven.

Beachy Head Lighthouse.

East Sussex is part of the historic county of Sussex which has its roots in the ancient kingdom of the South Saxons, who established themselves here in the fifth century AD after the departure of the Romans and archaeological remains are plentiful especially in the upland areas. The area's position on the south coast has meant that there were many early invaders including the Romans and Normans. Early industries included fishing, iron-making and the wool trade all of which have either declined or been lost completely.

East Sussex like most counties on the south coast has an annual average total of around 1570 hours of sunshine a year which is higher than the UK's average of about 1,340 hours per year. The coastline has promenades and piers, numerous attractions, fortifications, amusement arcades and of course many places to eat and drink.

Walking the coastline, particularly on top of the cliffs, means you are exposed to the elements whether it be wind and rain or direct sunlight on a hot sunny day. Remember to take suitable clothing including a cap if you are thin on top like me and refreshments, particularly if you are doing the longer cliff walks and don't forget your camera. The walks vary in length and difficulty but wherever possible, on the longer or harder walks, I have designed them so that you can do them as point-to-point walks or in two parts which will make them shorter and easier.

The East Sussex coast starts at Brighton and finishes at Camber on its famous sandy beach. Technically Brighton is an independent Borough; in 1997, as part of a local government reform, the borough of Hove merged with Brighton to form the Borough of Brighton and Hove and this authority was then granted city status in 2000. Although an independent borough it is classified as East Sussex for postal addresses. The borough of Brighton has its boundaries in Portslade and Saltdean so officially East Sussex starts in Saltdean. However, Brighton is the largest and arguably the most famous and popular location on the Sussex coast so it has been shared across both my books. In this volume is Part 2.

Detailed maps are not provided in the book but readers are recommended to refer to the relevant OS maps for the Sussex coast.

Brighton Marina.

Eastbourne seafront thanking the NHS.

CHAPTER 1
HOVE, BRIGHTON, ROTTINGDEAN & SALTDEAN (PT 2)

Brighton is a constituent part of the city of Brighton and Hove which were previously separate towns. It was in 1997 that the town of Brighton and its neighbouring town Hove were joined to form the unitary authority of Brighton and Hove, which was granted city status by Queen Elizabeth II as part of the millennium celebrations in 2000. Brighton and Hove is located to the east of Portslade and is in the county of East Sussex. Geographically the city of Brighton is considered part of East Sussex and it is referred to as such for postal addresses. However, in local authority terms East and West Sussex are separately run counties and Brighton is independent of them both as a unitary authority responsible for all its local government services. The Local Authority Boundary for Brighton and Hove is between Portslade and Saltdean along the south coast. As Brighton and Hove is so large with so many attractions, I ended my *West Sussex Coast* book here and featured a number of attractions in that book. This chapter focuses mainly on new attractions with two new walks but there will be a small amount of repetition so that this book can stand alone in its own right.

The beach at Brighton and Hove (from here just referred to as Brighton) is very famous and very popular with holidaymakers and day-trippers as Brighton train station is on a main line to London with all the intermediary stations on route making it easy to travel to. The beaches are pebbles interspersed with regular groynes. To the rear of the beach there is a popular cycle lane and Hove Lawns is a grassy area with many facilities

Amber cup.

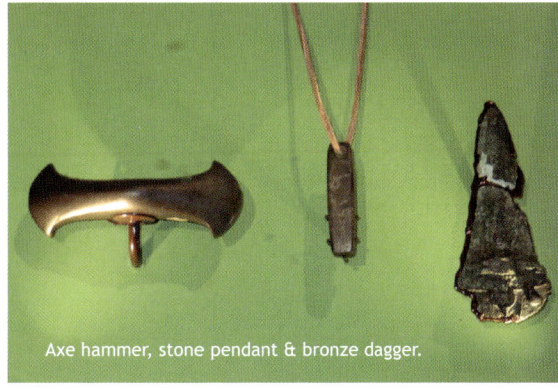
Axe hammer, stone pendant & bronze dagger.

along the Hove section as well as plenty of beach huts. Brighton has the cycle lane but the beach is overlooked mainly by hotels such as the Grand Hotel and the Hilton Metropole.

Hove was originally a small but ancient fishing village that was surrounded by farmland but it grew rapidly in the nineteenth century in response to the development of Brighton and by the Victorian era it was a fully developed town. Old spellings of Hove include Hou (Domesday Book), la Houue (1288), Huua (thirteenth century), Houve (13th and 14th centuries), Huve (14th and 15th centuries), Hova (sixteenth century) and Hoova (1675). No other places in Britain are called Hove and single-syllable names as a whole are rare in Sussex.

Fossilised remains from the Pleistocene era have been found in three locations in Hove. An 11lb 2oz (5kg) molar from Elephas antiguus was excavated from the garden of a house in Poplar Avenue, teeth from a juvenile elephant were found

Queen Victoria statue, Hove.

deep in the soil at Ventnor Villas and a prehistoric horse's tooth was found in the soil near Hove Street. During building work near Palmeira Square in 1856-57, workmen levelled a substantial burial mound; a prominent feature of the landscape since 1200 BC, the 20ft (6.1m) high tumulus yielded the Hove amber cup. Made of translucent red Baltic amber and about the same size as a regular china tea cup, the artefact has recently been relocated from the Hove Museum and is now displayed in the Brighton Museum & Art Gallery located in the grounds of the Royal Pavilion. Also buried in the coffin in which the amber cup was found were an axe hammer, a stone pendant and a bronze dagger which are also in the museum next to the amber cup; these items are 3600 years old.

A well-known reply by residents of Hove, usually humorous, when asked if they live in Brighton is "Hove, actually" thus maintaining a distinction with their less genteel neighbour. In the 1990s the Hove borough council used the slogan "Hove, actually" to promote the town for tourism.

At the seaward end of Grand Avenue is a bronze Grade II listed statue of Queen Victoria by Sir Thomas Brock. It was commissioned to celebrate the Queen's Jubilee in 1897 but it was not completed until 1901 by which time Victoria had unfortunately died. She is depicted as quite elderly, standing on a tall stone plinth and wrapped in a cloak. She is wearing a small crown and is holding a long sceptre and an orb on which stands a little winged figure of Victory, holding a trumpet and flaming torch. There is an inscription that reads: "Erected by the Inhabitants of Hove to Commemorate the 60th Anniversary of the Accession of Queen Victoria June 20 AD 1897".

There is archaeological evidence of a settlement at Brighton that dates back to the Bronze Age, Roman and Anglo-Saxon periods. The ancient settlement of Brighthelmstone was documented in the Domesday Book (1086). The town's importance grew in the Middle Ages as the Old Town developed but it languished in the early modern period, affected by foreign attacks, storms, a suffering economy and a declining population. Brighton started to attract more visitors following improved road transport to London and after becoming a boarding point for boats sailing to France; it also became popular as a health resort for bathing as a believed cure for illnesses.

In Georgian times Brighton developed as a fashionable seaside resort which was encouraged by the patronage of the Prince Regent, later King George IV, who spent much time in the town and constructed the Royal Pavilion in the Regency era. Brighton continued to grow following the arrival of the railways in 1841. Many of the major attractions were built in the Victorian era including the Grand Hotel, the Hilton Metropole, the Palace Pier and the West Pier. The town continued to grow into the twentieth century expanding to incorporate more areas into the towns boundaries before joining with Hove.

The Royal Pavilion which is also known as the Brighton Pavilion is a Grade I listed former Royal residence. Beginning in 1787 it was built in three stages, as a seaside retreat for George, Prince of Wales, who became Prince Regent in 1811 and

Royal Pavilion.

King George IV in 1820. It is built in the Indo-Saracenic style prevalent in India for most of the nineteenth century. The current appearance of the Pavilion, with its domes and minarets is the work of architect John Nash who extended the building starting in 1815. George IV's successors William IV and Victoria also used the Pavilion but Queen Victoria decided that Osborne House on the Isle of Wight should be the royal seaside retreat and the Pavilion was sold to the city of Brighton in 1850. On 1st April 2020 management and operation of the Royal Pavilion & Museums' buildings and collections were transferred from Brighton & Hove City Council to a new charity – the Royal Pavilion & Museums Trust (RPMT). The purchase of the Royal Pavilion from Queen Victoria marked the beginnings of the site's attraction as a tourist destination. The Royal Pavilion has been changed from a private residence to a public attraction under civic ownership and around 400,000 people visit annually. When visiting the Pavilion look out for the Prince of Wales' emblem (feathers) at the front on the central dome and the bronze statue of George IV which is by the North Gate; it was sculpted by Sir Francis Chantrey and was originally sited in 1828.

The 'Golden Gallopers' carousel has been on Brighton seafront every summer since 1997. The word 'carousel' is believed to derive from the Spanish carosella which means 'little war' and was probably named after a Turkish game played by soldiers on horseback. The 'Golden Gallopers' on Brighton seafront was built in 1888 by Frederick Savage at his workshop in King's Lynn. At the start of its life, it toured the North of England for over twenty years before being bought by an

Prince of Wales' emblem on central dome.

American enthusiast who shipped it to the USA. It was returned to England in 1990 when it was bought and restored by Mr Corbin of Wiltshire. The current owner, Owen Smith, bought the carousel in 1997 and it has been on Brighton seafront from Easter to September every year since. At the end of each season, it is de-constructed for six months of essential renovation and repairs; repainting and re-varnishing is also carried out. The carousel is a popular attraction and has featured in many films.

'Golden Gallopers' on Brighton Beach.

Left: George IV by North Gate.

Brighton Marina is an artificial marina that features a working harbour and residential housing alongside leisure, retail and commercial activities. The marina covers an area of about 127 acres (0.51 km2) and was constructed between 1971 and 1979 but there have been continuous developments ever since. The marina was opened for use in 1978 but was officially opened by Queen Elizabeth II on 31 May 1979. The land cost £50,000 to purchase and between then and 1996 the marina's value increased substantially when in 1996 Brunswick Developments purchased the marina for £9m. The marina offers food from almost every type of cuisine, luxury hotels which sit next to independent shops, a cinema, bowling, bars and much more. It is a major attraction for boat lovers and if you time your arrival right on most winter evenings before dusk you can witness thousands of starlings returning from across the Sussex countryside to roost beneath the Wetherspoons pub or on the Palace or West Piers. Known as a murmuration the starlings can be seen anywhere along the seafront and on a calm evening you can even hear the flutter of their wings as they swoop in to roost.

East Breakwater from Undercliff.

Brighton Marina.

Volks Electric Railway on Brighton's seafront is over 138 years old and is the oldest electric railway in the world that is still in operation. It was invented by Magnus Volk (1851-1937) who was an enthusiastic inventor. As a young man he liked to build machines and experiment with electricity and soon became an expert in all things electrical. In 1879 he brought the first telephone system to Brighton which he installed in his house and that of his friend, William Jago. A year later, at the age of twenty-nine, he was the first person on the south coast of England to fit electric lights in his house.

Volks Electric Railway (VER).

His most famous innovations were in railways and in 1883 he decided to build a small line running along the seafront in Brighton using electricity to power the trains. It opened on 4 August 1883 and is still in operation today. As soon as the railway was up and running Magnus wanted to extend it further into town but unfortunately the Corporation would not give him permission to do this so he extended it to the east instead. As it continued to grow in popularity, new carriages were added to increase capacity. In 1901 it was extended again out to Black Rock and was now 1.25 miles in total. The service still runs taking passengers on a nostalgic journey between the Palace Pier and Black Rock by Brighton Marina. (A journey you can make on walk 1.)

The Chattri Memorial is a war memorial on the South Downs. During WWI injured Indian soldiers were hospitalised in the Royal Pavilion, Dome and Corn Exchange. The Royal Pavilion was the first Indian hospital to open in Brighton and the Hindus and Sikhs who died were cremated on the Downs; in 1921 the Chattri Memorial was constructed on the cremation site.

Chattri War Memorial.

The memorial commemorates 53 men of the Indian Army who died and were cremated at Patcham Down during WWI; this was in accordance with Hindu and Sikh religious rites. The soldiers were transferred to hospital in Brighton after fighting on the Western Front from 1914-15. The graves of the Muslim soldiers who died in Brighton are in Brookwood Military Cemetery in Surrey. The inscription on the memorial written in Hindi, Punjabi and English

Inscription on memorial.   Names of the 53 men who died.

reads 'In honour of these soldiers of the Indian Army whose mortal remains were committed to fire'.

The Chattri Memorial was unveiled by the Prince of Wales in 1921 with the inscription: 'To the memory of all the Indian soldiers who gave their lives for their King-Emperor in the Great War, this monument, erected on the site of the funeral pyre where the Hindus and Sikhs who died in hospital at Brighton, passed through the fire, is in grateful admiration and brotherly affection dedicated'. The memorial is visited on walk 2.

Roedean School is a famous independent day and boarding school for girls aged eleven to eighteen located in Roedean Village on the outskirts of Brighton. The campus is situated near the Sussex Downs on a cliff overlooking Brighton Marina and the English Channel. The school has dance studios, music classrooms, a 320-seat theatre, a heated indoor swimming pool, golf course, farm and a chapel as well as a range of workshops, studios, laboratories and sports pitches.

Roedean School perched high above the cliffs.

The school was founded in 1885 as Wimbledon House by three sisters – Penelope, Millicent and Dorothy Lawrence; their brother was the lawyer Sir Paul Lawrence of Wimbledon who helped them considerably. The school motto, *Honneur aulx dignes*, is in Norman French and means 'Honour the worthy' and when pronounced it sounds like 'Honour Roedean'. The school is passed on walk 3.

ROTTINGDEAN

Rottingdean is a village that borders Saltdean, Ovingdean and Woodingdean. It is located in a dry valley whose sides in the upper reaches are quite steep and the valley comes right down to the English Channel.

The name Rottingdean means 'valley of Rota's people' (a male personal name). It is likely that Rota was the leader of a band of Saxons who invaded the region in 450-500 AD and who replaced the existing Romano-British inhabitants. The first recorded mention is in the Domesday Book as Rotingeden 1086 and at the time of the Domesday Book the village had around 50 to 100 inhabitants. Other variations of the place name to be found in ancient charters include Ruttingedene 1272, Rottyngden 1315 and Rottendeane 1673.

Within the parish lies the deserted hamlet of Balsdean and the adjacent village of Woodingdean was until 1933 part of the Rottingdean parish. Also, formerly in the parish was most of the district of what is now Saltdean.

The first settlers of Rottingdean were the Neolithic (New Stone Age) people who arrived around 2500 BC. They would have cut down trees and scrub to make fields for growing cereals such as barley. Through the ages from Neolithic to Bronze Age, from Roman to Anglo-Saxon the same fields were probably worked. A Bronze-Age barrow (a mound of earth and stones raised over a grave) and pottery fragments were found when houses were being built in the area now known as Rottingdean Heights and on the other side of the village an Iron-Age burial site was uncovered in 1863 on Beacon Hill. A Saxon warrior grave complete with sword was found during the digging of Rottingdean windmill's foundations.

The Celtic Iron Age mode of life probably continued unchanged after the arrival of the Romans in 43AD but from the middle of the third century, people living near the coast were terrorized by Saxon raiders. Some wealthy Romano-Britons took their money from their villas and buried it in pots on remote downland sites. One such hoard was unearthed at Balsdean which contained over a thousand coins dating from 275-287. After the Romans withdrew from Britain, Saxons started to settle in Sussex, the name Sussex being derived from the land of the South Saxons.

Most histories of Rottingdean say that its habitants were involved in smuggling. The smuggling was in both directions with wool being smuggled out and tea, spirits, tobacco and lace being smuggled in. A number of documented seizures of contraband were made in Rottingdean in the second half of the eighteen century. The contraband was probably unloaded at Saltdean Gap as it was a more deserted spot. It would then be transported over the hill, down the present Whiteway Lane into the village and then taken inland for distribution. Local stories claim that there were secret passages under the village. These stories cannot be proved but it is consistently rumoured that in the eighteenth century vicar Dr Thomas Hooker was involved. However, the other side of Hooker was his devotion to education and he opened schools in the village both for the rich and for the local children.

Rottingdean was once a centre for hunting especially in the second half of the nineteenth century; the Brookside Hunt was based in the village until 1902 which hunted hares and foxes with a pack of hounds.

Rottingdean is well known for its black wooden windmill which sits prominently on Beacon Hill. The smock windmill was erected in 1802 by Thomas Beard and he carved the initials TB 1802 on an internal timber. A curious incident was reported in the *Sussex Weekly Advertiser* of 7 June 1802: on digging the foundations, workmen uncovered the remains of an ancient warrior and sword. When they returned after a break, both items had gone and were never seen again!

The mill ground corn for the village and supplied flour to local bakers. Around 1877 George Nicholls was miller and baker and his son Harry would deliver hot rolls around the village before school. They lived in the High Street and George was the last miller when the mill ceased to function in 1881. The mill was still in operation in 1880 when Georgiana Burne-Jones (wife of the famous painter Sir Edward Coley Burne-Jones 1833-1898) first came to Rottingdean, as she recorded that 'the sails of the windmill were turning slowly in the sun and the miller's black timber cottage was still there'.

Once it stopped working, the mill became increasingly dilapidated; it was damaged by fire, lost its sweeps and fantails, and gaping holes appeared in its wooden sides. By 1922 when the village realised that they were likely to lose their mill altogether a parish meeting was called and £400 was raised for repairs, with one of their distinguished supporters being Hilaire Belloc (British-French writer and historian and one of the most prolific writers in England during the early twentieth century).

Rottingdean Windmill.

The next year the Marquis of Abergavenny, Lord of the Manor, granted a 99-year lease of the mill and the trustees agreed 'not to alter or detract from the picturesque appearance of the mill, and to preserve the same as an object of interest to the inhabitants and visitors to Rottingdean and district'. In 1929 the mill was re-tarred and basic repairs carried out. In 1935 Fred Neve made the mill weatherproof and safe for many years, the work being funded by Mr Yapp of Haywards Heath. It was strengthened enough to take a new set of sweeps.

When the Rottingdean Preservation Society was formed in

1960 the trusteeship of the mill was vested in members of the Society together with a full repairing lease. Between 1961-65 further repairs were made including timber treatment against beetles and the base was re-tarred. Soon after, gales damaged the sweeps, the mill was struck by lightning, and in 1969, a steel framework was erected inside the mill to stop it twisting and collapsing. The work was carried out by Ernest Hole and Son at a cost of £3500; fortunately, the Society received a substantial bequest from Mr R. A. Caton at about that time to make this and future work possible.

In the 1980s, on the advice of the Society for the Protection of Ancient Buildings, the sweeps were removed and the weight of the upper structure transferred on to the steel frame. From that time virtually the whole mill was supported by the internal steelwork and in 1987 the mill withstood the infamous hurricane without any significant damage. Subsequent work required a significant amount of oak and included a donation of an English oak tree by Lord March of Goodwood.

As part of the Millennium project, the Preservation Society replaced three of the eight wooden cant posts, some internal frames and feather-boarding, and weatherproofed the cap at a total cost to the Society of over £57,000. In 2003 the sweeps and stocks needed replacement and this was supported by a grant from the Heritage Lottery Fund. Work is ongoing on this Grade II listed landmark as it is constantly battered by the prevailing south-westerly winds. Constant attention and maintenance is carried out by the Rottingdean Preservation Society. The mill is open to the public on National Mills Days and regularly throughout the summer. Rottingdean Windmill is passed on walk 3.

Beacon Hill Nature Reserve in Rottingdean has been a designated nature reserve since 2005. The area of chalk grassland is on the edge of the South Downs and the flower rich grassland and shrubby edged woodland is home to a variety of wildlife. Once covering much of the South Downs, chalk grassland is now a rare habitat and this area supports a range of insects, birds, mammals and reptiles. Over 25 species of butterfly including common blues, meadow browns, marbled whites and dark green fritillaries are seen in the summer and on occasion the rare Adonis blue. In late summer the distinctive wasp spider with its zig-zag web pops up in the brambles and common lizards can be seen here.

Skylarks are heard throughout the year and the residents are joined by migratory birds in the spring and the males can be seen hovering high in the sky, singing to mark their territory before parachuting down to the ground where they nest. Seasonal visitors include swallows, martins and swifts and the odd kestrel may be spotted or at dusk an owl. In the woods and scrub on the eastern boundary whitethroat, chiffchaff, blackcap, goldfinch and stock dove breed and tits use the woodland nest boxes.

Plants to look out for include cowslips, yellow rattle, lady's bedstraw, knapweeds, pyramidal orchids and the county flower of Sussex the round-headed rampion after which the offshore Rampion Wind Farm is named.

SALTDEAN

Saltdean is a coastal village that contains the official eastern boundary to Brighton and Hove, with East Saltdean lying outside the city boundary in Lewes District. Saltdean is about 5 miles (8 km) east of central Brighton and 6 miles (9.7 km) south of Lewes and is bordered by the South Downs National Park. It is situated by the sea in a 'Dean' (Saxon/Old English for 'dry valley'), with the surrounding hills of the South Downs forming a large central dip and valley where the oval-shaped Saltdean Park and Lido are located.

Saltdean was open farmland and originally part of Rottingdean and almost uninhabited until 1924 when land was sold off for speculative housing and property development. Some of this was promoted by Charles W. Neville who had set up a company to develop the site; he also eventually built nearby Peacehaven and parts of Rottingdean.

Saltdean has a mainly shingle beach fronted by the Undercliff Walk which can be reached from the cliff top by steps from the coast road; the Undercliff Walk continues to Brighton ending by the Palace Pier. The best-known building is the Grade II listed Saltdean Lido community centre, which includes a public library and iconic open air swimming pool, designed by architect R.W.H. Jones.

Now you can do the three associated walks – between the Palace Pier and Brighton Marina (maybe cheating and using Volks Electric Railway), Chattri War Memorial on the South Downs and Rottingdean Windmill, Roedean School and Undercliff. I will see you in Chapter 2 where we explore Telscombe and visit the Meridian Marker.

Undercliff Walk

SUGGESTED WALK

WALK 1. Palace Pier to Brighton Marina & Pavilion (6 miles 9.7 km)

Parking. Park wherever you want in Brighton or arrive by train or bus. This is a fairly flat walk with a gentle climb between the marina up to Marine Parade. Refreshments are available throughout the walk.

1. With your back to Brighton Palace Pier turn right and walk eastwards along the seafront towards Brighton Marina in sight. In 150 yards you reach Volks Electric Railway and you have a choice to make, either continue walking along Madeira Drive or jump on the train and go in style. Just continue along passing the famous arches on the left (possibly fenced off for safety reasons) and a statue of Steve Ovett, the British gold medal runner who was born in Brighton. When you reach Black Rock (this is where the train ends and it is further on than the workshop area) continue ahead to the marina and look out for the sign above a short underpass saying 'Welcome to Brighton Marina'. (At the time of writing this area was undergoing a lot of development so the layout may change slightly). Go through the underpass and straight ahead on the right-hand side of a car park, you are aiming for the ASDA supermarket ahead. When you reach ASDA by a roundabout go right along a short road and in a few yards go up the wide set of steps to reach a Wetherspoons pub that overlooks the marina.

Brighton Palace Pier.

Famous arches and railings.

2. Go left by the pub and walk along the left-hand side of the marina passing numerous restaurants and then continue with residential flats on your left. On the far side cross over East Lockside and continue for a few yards to reach the marina's East Breakwater. Now do a there-and-back walk along the East Breakwater to enjoy views back across the marina and you also get a good view of Roedean girls' school perched high up on the top of the cliffs a little further east along the seafront. Now return to East Lockside and just before it go right and in 30 yards go left over the lock and follow the road ahead between residential flats and then retail outlets to arrive back at ASDA. (The retail outlets are worth looking around.) Go past

Brighton Marina.

East Lockside.

ASDA and continue ahead through their car park and on the far side go right up steps then go left under the road (not through the tunnel). Go along a gravel path and in 50 yards go up a flight of steps to reach the main road – Marine Parade.

3. Go left along the road, immediately crossing Dukes Mound and continue while enjoying the views. When you reach the fourth set of pedestrian lights (which are quite close to the pier) cross over and go ahead up Lower Rock Gardens directly opposite. At the top go left along St James Street, not signed, and follow it to its end passing shops as you go. At the end you can see the Palace Pier to your left but you need to go ahead crossing two roads and on the far side go right to reach the Brighton Pavilion. Follow the perimeter fence around until you reach the North Gate by a statue of George IV. Enter the grounds here to visit the Pavilion and Brighton Museum & Art Gallery which is on your right near the entrance which now houses the Hove amber cup and the axe hammer, stone pendant and bronze dagger that were all found inside an oak coffin in Hove in 1856. (Ask one of the staff at the reception to show you where the amber cup is as it is hard to find. It is in the Elaine Evans Archaeology Gallery in a very small blacked-out display case and the cup comes to life when you press a button that makes a light shine through the cup showing its amber beauty. The other artefacts are in the display directly to the left of the cup. My thanks to Adrienn Nemeth who showed me the location of the cup and who patiently pressed the light button so that I could get my photo).

Brighton Museum & Art Gallery.

Brighton Pavilion.

Once you have visited the Pavilion and museum return to the same entrance. Follow the perimeter fence back, recross left over the road then turn right to the pier in sight back to the start.

SUGGESTED WALK

WALK 2. Chattri War Memorial (2.25 miles 3.6 km)

Parking. There is limited roadside parking along Braypool Lane; this is a small slip-road that is accessed from a roundabout. Immediately turn right along the lane and park on the LHS about 50-100 yards along the lane. This is a slightly hilly walk but it is a gradual climb, not steep; there are no stiles. (what3words – frog.sweat.quick.) Chattri Memorial can only be reached on foot and this walk is a there-and-back walk that deliberately follows the route that people walk on the official days of memorial services.

1. A little further along from the parking area, on the brow of a hill at a junction, go left up an access lane. In 15 yards go through a bridle gate by a two-way footpath sign. Go ahead up the middle of a field on a faint grassy path and soon you will see the white-domed memorial in the distance behind a clump of trees. Go through a bridle gate and along a left field edge with a wire fence on your left. At the end of the fence the path starts to curve around to the right. Pass a three-way signpost and in about 120 yards you reach trees over to the right, go over and walk beside them and you arrive by the entrance gate to the Chattri War Memorial. Explore the memorial, read the inscription on the lower left-hand side of the memorial and take the time to appreciate the view that the memorial enjoys, including the British airways i360 Observation Tower on Brighton seafront. ('Chattri' is Hindi, Punjabi and Urdu for umbrella and this is not only reflected in its design but also symbolises the protection offered to the memory of the dead.)

Chattri War Memorial.

2. Leave by the same gate and return the same way as people have to do on official days of memorial services.

Left: View to Brighton.

SUGGESTED WALK

WALK 3. Rottingdean Windmill, Roedean School and Undercliff
(5.25 miles 8.4 km)

Parking. There is roadside parking by the Plough Inn pub or in a nearby side road including Dean Court Road (Post Code BN2 7HD - Pub). This is quite a hilly walk with a couple of short steep climbs and there are two stiles. Refreshments are available from the Plough Inn and numerous shops or pubs in Rottingdean High Street.

1. With your back to the Plough Inn go right down the road and at the end go left down the High Street. In 20 yards cross over and go right up Nevill Road. Go ahead and climb quite steeply, soon passing to the right of a low stone wall which goes across part of the road. In 15 yards go right along Sheep Walk and enter Beacon Hill Nature Reserve. Go directly ahead and just before a bench go left along a narrow path to reach Rottingdean Windmill. From the mill go right uphill on a wide grassy path to reach a stone pillar in about 50 yards that was 'erected by Rottingdean Branch and women's section of the Royal British Legion in April 2000 to celebrate the Millennium' which commemorates various historical events. From this

The Plough Inn.

Rottingdean Windmill.

spot take a while to enjoy the panoramic views including the Rampion Wind Farm out at sea (the name Rampion being taken from the county flower of Sussex that grows in this area). From here go left and follow the grassy path walking parallel with the sea away on your left. Just follow the path and go left immediately behind a large building. Go through a gate and down an enclosed path to reach a road.

2. Turn right along the right-hand pavement to reach Ovingdean by Beacon Hill (a road) on the right. Directly opposite Beacon Hill go left through a bridle gate by a footpath sign. Now go ahead up and over Cattle Hill following a wire

Millennium pillar.

fence on your right at first and then it's on your left after going through a bridle gate. Pass a cylindrical brick column and soon you get a good view of the rear of the famous Roedean Girls School and the East Breakwater of Brighton Marina which you walked along on walk 1.

Cross a stile and continue behind the school then descend steeply down some steps, over a stile then on to reach Roedean Way. Go left (not into the school) along a left field edge to reach the main Marine Drive at the end with the front of Roedean School on your left. Cross the road and turn right along the pavement to reach a set of traffic lights. (There are good views of the marina from here).

Roedean Girls School.

3. Go left at the lights, down a concrete access road, go around a barrier and down to reach the Undercliff Walk. Now follow the Undercliff Walk for about a mile remembering to look back towards the marina to get a photo of the marina with the steep white cliffs. Pass the first exit which is a flight of steps and continue to the second exit which is a ramp by Highcliff Court; it also says Rottingdean. Exit here and go ahead up the High Street opposite. (There are a lot of picturesque shops, bars, cafés etc in this area that are worth visiting.) Go along the High Street for about 180 yards then turn right up Vicarage Lane back to the Plough Inn for refreshments back at the start.

Access to Undercliff Walk.

Undercliff Walk back to Brighton Marina (East Breakwater).

CHAPTER 2
TELSCOMBE & PEACEHAVEN

TELSCOMBE

Telscombe is a civil parish and electoral ward (called East Saltdean and Telscombe Cliffs) with the status of a town in the Lewes District of East Sussex. It consists of three settlements separated from each other by an open area of downland called Telscombe Tye.

Telscombe village is a small village on the South Downs 6 miles south of Lewes and includes the parish church with origins dating back to the tenth century. The ancient parish boundaries reach from the village to the coast where the major part of its population is in the two coastal settlements. At the eastern end of the parish the majority of the population live at Telscombe Cliffs which was developed in the twentieth century effectively as an extension of Peacehaven over the town boundary. At the western end the remaining population forms part of the community of Saltdean, the remainder of Saltdean, as previously explained in Chapter 1, being within the City of Brighton and Hove.

The parish includes part of the Brighton to Newhaven Cliffs Site of Special Scientific Interest (SSSI); the cliffs being mainly of geological interest as they contain many Santonian and Campanian fossils. The SSSI listing also includes flora and fauna biological interest as well.

Telscombe Cliffs.

The manor of Telscombe was recorded in the tenth century when it was given by King Edgar (c943 – 8 July 975 and known as the Peaceful or the Peaceable) to the minster of Hyde and it remained in those hands until the dissolution of the monasteries in 1538. Over the centuries the manor and village passed through many hands; in 1900 James Andrew Harman became Lord of the Manor and in 1924 it was acquired by Charles William Neville, the developer who had founded Peacehaven in 1916. The village was part of the Holmstrow Hundred (administrative unit in the Rape of Lewes) until the abolition of hundreds in the nineteenth century.

Telscombe Village is just under 2 miles (3 km) from the coast and only contains a small cluster of buildings around a church dedicated to St Laurence. It is a tenth century foundation with a thirteenth century font, largely rebuilt and decorated in the twentieth century. The manor house was for many years used as a Judge's Lodgings that was occupied when High Court judges were sitting at Lewes Crown Court. This practice was controversial because of the costs of providing and maintaining this accommodation, including the employment of butlers and other staff and was phased out by a Labour government from 2001.

Telscombe Tye is an area of open land extending from Telscombe village to the coast that forms a natural break between the settlements of Saltdean

St Laurence's church, Telscombe Village.

and Telscombe Cliffs / Peacehaven and it marks the eastern end of the continuously built-up area (Greater Brighton) from Shoreham in West Sussex. The Tye is contained within the South Downs National Park and is one of only a few places where the park boundary reaches the coast. As designated common the land was unenclosed and, on a map, dated 1811 it was shown as 'Sheep Down' on which local stockholders had grazing rights. One such landowner in the early twentieth century was Ambrose Gorham who managed a stud farm and trained racehorses including the 1902 winner of the Grand National – Shannon Lass, trained by James Hackett, ridden by David Read in a time of 10 min 3.6 sec.

PEACEHAVEN

Peacehaven is a town in the Lewes District of East Sussex. It is located above the chalk cliffs of the South Downs and its location coincides with the point where the Greenwich Meridian crosses the south coast. Peacehaven is next to Telscombe Cliffs which is a later extension to Peacehaven that lies within a separate parish and has a separate town council.

A Bronze Age barrow (burial mound) lies close to the cliff top which has been studied by local societies and it gives evidence of the occupation of Peacehaven to at least 3500 years ago. A 2007 excavation of the new Bovis Homes site to the west of Peacehaven Community School's playing fields unearthed a large range of evidence for a prehistoric settlement throughout the Bronze and Iron Ages.

The process and evolution of naming Peacehaven was far more complicated than it might first appear. First established in 1916 the name was chosen through a series of competitions run by Charles Neville in nearly all the local and national newspapers. Neville would choose the winning name and whoever had submitted it would receive £100 and a free plot of land. The winning name was 'New Anzac-on-Sea' which was chosen to commemorate the ANZAC's involvement in the Battle of Gallipoli. The *Daily Express* later sued Neville over the competition, holding that it was a scam, since he was offering 'free' plots of land in the town as runner-up prizes but issuing them only on the payment of a conveyancing fee of £3

Waves and stones crash over the Undercliff Walk in strong winds.

and 3 shillings; 2000 people took up the offer. A three-year set of court cases between the *Daily Express* and Neville went as high as the House of Lords, the highest court in the land, which was won by the *Daily Express*. The result was immaterial in the end as on the 12 February 1917 it was renamed Peacehaven and was a huge success thanks to the court case publicity.

The town was originally formed for retiring WWI veterans in order for them to escape and recover from the effects of the war as the setting, sea air and simple lifestyle was thought to have aided good health. The land was cheap and working-class families from the city started to purchase plots and gradually build makeshift homes for weekends and holidays; this movement of frontier-style buildings made from whatever materials were available at the time was termed as the Plotlands movement.

By 1924 there were 3000 people living in Peacehaven, the original houses were often very temporary; some were old railway carriages and others were constructed from former army huts, brought from North Camp near Seaford. Eventually the local council invested in water and electrical services and so people started to build more substantial houses.

Meridian Marker.

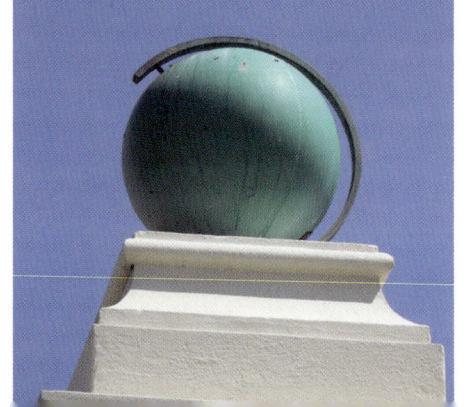

Peacehaven is located on fairly flat coastal land that is elevated to about 40-50m (131-164 ft) above sea level. The pebble beach below the cliffs can be accessed by stairs and concrete driveway. The parish includes part of the Brighton to Newhaven Cliffs Site of Special Scientific Interest. The Prime Meridian is marked by a 3.5m (11.5 ft) tall obelisk that was commissioned by Charles Neville. It was unveiled on 10 August 1936 and has been relocated twice due to cliff erosion. The obelisk was damaged in the storms in 1987 when its globe on top was lost to the sea; it has since been replaced. There is a plaque on the obelisk as follows:

Meridian Marker.

PEACEHAVEN

KING GEORGE V. MEMORIAL

ERECTED BY THE INHABITANTS IN THE YEAR 1936 TO COMMEMORATE THE BENEFICENT AND ILLUSTRIOUS REIGN OF THEIR BELOVED-SOVERIGN (1910-1936) AND TO MARK PEACEHAVEN'S POSITION ON THE PRIME MERIDIAN OF GREENWICH

The popular singer and comedian Dame Gracie Fields bought a home in Peacehaven overlooking the sea and then established the Gracie Fields Home and Orphanage in Dorothy Avenue. In fact, the children were not actually orphans; their parents were entertainers who placed their children there while they were on tour. It was administered by the Theatrical Ladies Guild and Dorothy House is now a care home for the elderly.

Now you can do the associated walk which has been designed so that you visit Telscombe Village, Tye and Cliffs before reaching the Meridian Marker in Peacehaven. I will see you at Newhaven when we visit Newhaven Fort, walk beside the River Ouse and look at the fish on Piddinghoe church.

SUGGESTED WALK

WALK 4. Telscombe Church and Meridian Monument (6 miles 9.7 km)

Parking. There is 'considerate' residential roadside parking at the top of Roderick Avenue/Roderick Avenue North (Post Code BN10 8JG). This is a hilly walk with a couple of long and very steep climbs one of them being at the very end up through Peacehaven but there are no stiles. Refreshments are available from the Smugglers Rest or the Telscombe Tavern en-route or shops along South Coast Road.

1. (The walk starts at the very end of the residential part of Roderick Avenue North.) From the end of the road go ahead past the speed limit signs along an access road which is actually still part of Roderick Avenue North. Go left along Valley Road soon passing Gold Lane on the left. At the end go right along a narrower access track and at the end go left along a path between trees at first then with open views especially to the right. At the end you arrive at St Laurence's church in Telscombe Village.

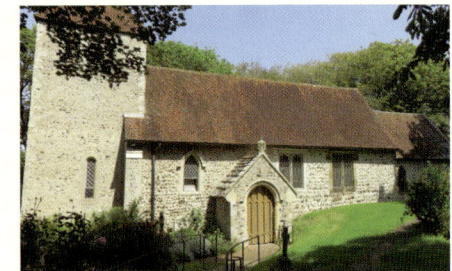
St Laurence's church.

2. From the church go left along the road beside the church and climb steeply. At the top go ahead to the right of a cattle grid, through a bridle gate, to reach a four-way signpost. Go ahead along a gravelled track and in 30 yards continue ahead along a grass / gravelled track. (You are now walking across Telscombe Tye with Saltdean on your right and Peacehaven on your left.) Just keep going, dodging the many sheep (on a map dated 1811 this area was shown as 'sheep Down') and on the far side go through a bridle gate out to the main road at Telscombe

Telscombe Cliffs weather vane.

Cliffs. Cross the main South Coast Road and detour to the right for 100 yards to reach the Telscombe Cliffs Weather Vane. It was erected in 1995 to mark fifty years from the end of WWII.

Eroding cliff near Smugglers Rest pub.

3. Now return back and head east, with the sea on your right, we are now heading for the Meridian Marker which is about one and a quarter miles away. Due to significant cliff erosion the exact route may change a little over time but just walk as close as you can to the safety fences and follow the signposts. Alternatively you can walk along the pavement but beside the fence is much better; either way you can't miss the Marker.

Just keep going and soon you reach the Smugglers Rest pub which is ideally located for refreshments. The path runs behind the pub and here there are a set of steps which give you access to the beach from where you get a good view of the eroding cliffs. (You are warned about the potential for falling material.)

Continue ahead and soon you will see the Meridian Marker in the distance directly ahead of you on top of a hill. Just keep going until you reach the information board and Meridian Marker, the point at which the Greenwich Meridian leaves the south coast. The Greenwich Meridian separates east from west in the same way that the equator separates north from south. Inextricably linked with Greenwich Mean Time, it also sits at the centre of our system of time zones. Its path is determined by the location of an historic telescope, the Airy Transit circle, which is housed at the Royal Observatory, Greenwich.

From the Meridian Monument go left along Horsham Avenue. At the end cross over and go left along the main South Coast Road. Pass Roderick Avenue on your right and continue to a roundabout. Turn right up Sutton Avenue and follow it as it curves to the right then automatically filters into Roderick Avenue (Roderick Avenue was not continuous down to the main road). Now just continue walking ahead uphill, the road undulates and at one point you have to pass between a barrier, and eventually you arrive back at the junction of Roderick Avenue/ Roderick Avenue North at the start.

Meridian Marker.

CHAPTER 3
NEWHAVEN & PIDDINGHOE

Newhaven is a channel ferry port that operates regular Transmanche ferries to Dieppe. It lies at the mouth of the River Ouse which has historically migrated westward from Seaford. A breakwater was built at the village of Meeching and a new outlet was cut through the valley. In 1847 the railway reached the port enabling a train-to-ferry which brought great activity and the area became known as the 'New Haven', and was officially recognised as 'The Port of Newhaven' in 1882.

River Ouse at Newhaven.

There was a Bronze Age fort on what is now Castle Hill and in about 480 A.D., the Saxon people established a village near to where Newhaven now stands which they named "Meeching" (also called "Myching" or "Mitching"). Throughout the Middle Ages the main outlet and port of the River Ouse was at Seaford – one of the Cinque Ports (a historic group of coastal towns in Kent, Sussex and Essex).

The growth of the shingle spit impeded the outflow of the River Ouse which consequently flooded the Levels upstream and hindered access to the port. A channel was cut through the shingle spit in the mid-16th century below Castle Hill, creating access to a sheltered harbour that was better than Seaford; this was the origin of modern Newhaven. However, the shingle continued to accumulate and so the mouth of the Ouse began to migrate eastwards again. Under the Ouse Navigation Act 1790, a western breakwater was constructed to arrest longshore drift and so cut off the supply of shingle to the spit. A new outlet, The Cut, was built on the river's present course, below Castle Hill. The present breakwater was built in 1880.

The village was of little maritime importance until the opening of the railway line to Lewes in 1847. In 1848 the exiled French King Louis Philippe landed here in disguise after abdicating his throne. The London Brighton and South Coast Railway (LB&SCR) constructed their own wharf and facilities on the east side of the River Ouse and opened the Newhaven harbour railway station. The railway also funded the dredging of the channel and made other improvements to the harbour between 1850-1878, to enable it to be used by cross channel ferries. In 1863 the LB&SCR and the Chemin de Fer de l'Ouest introduced the Newhaven-Dieppe passenger service. The harbour was officially recognised as 'The Port of Newhaven' in 1882 and imports at that time included French farm products, timber, granite and slates.

Newhaven Ferry Port.

The harbour was designated as the principal port for the movement of men and material to the European continent during WWI and it was taken over by the military authorities and the ferries requisitioned for the duration of the war. Between 22 September 1916 and 2 December 1918, the port and town were designated a 'Special Military Area' under the 'Defence of the Realm Regulations' and the harbour was closed to the public. The port and harbour facilities, rail sidings and warehousing were enlarged at this time and electric lighting installed to allow for 24-hour operation. During WWII, large numbers of Canadian troops were stationed at Newhaven and the ill-fated Dieppe Raid in 1942 was largely launched from the harbour.

The port is the proposed main landside site for E.ON's development of the offshore Rampion Wind Farm. Newhaven Marina provided berthing facilities, fuel and other services for the crew transfer vessels working on the construction of the wind farm.

When the high-profile gambler and murder-suspect Lord Lucan vanished in 1974 his car was found abandoned in Norman Road, Newhaven, with traces of blood matching the blood-groups of his children's nanny Sandra Rivett, whom he is believed to have murdered and his wife, whom he had attempted to murder, according to her testimony. The Newhaven location suggested that he had taken the cross-channel ferry but no confirmed sightings of him were ever made.

The Newhaven Lifeboat, the first of which was commissioned in 1803 is among the oldest in Britain and was established some twenty years before the Royal National Lifeboat Institution. The town established the rescue lifeboat in response to the wreck of HMS *Brazen* in January 1800 when only one man of the crew of 105 men could be saved.

Newhaven Fort is one of the Palmerston Forts (also known as Palmerston's Follies) and was built on Castle Hill on the recommendation of the 1859 Royal Commission to defend the growing harbour; it was the largest defence work ever built in Sussex and is now a museum. The fort was one of 72 coastal forts to be

Newhaven Fort.

commissioned by the British Government under Lord Palmerston, in response to the apparently threatening behaviour of Napoleon III who was busy building his navy and strengthening his own coastal defences. It was designed by twenty-two-year-old John Charles Ardagh of the Royal Engineers and construction began in 1862 and took ten years and 6 million bricks to complete.

By the end of the nineteenth Century the fort needed updating and was practically rebuilt; new modern guns were installed and baths for the soldiers. During WWI the harbour shipped six million tons of supplies to France so this meant that the Fort established itself as part of a larger network of defences that included gunboats, thousands of soldiers and a seaplane based in Seaford Bay.

When WWII broke out in 1939, Newhaven Fort was a vital element in the defence against the very real threat of a German invasion. A coastal radar site was built just outside the Fort, linked to a large underground naval communication centre nearby. In the harbour were gunboats, minesweepers and boats of the RAF Air Sea Rescue, whose soldiers used part of the Fort as a rest area. Post-war, the last unit to be stationed here was the Ukrainians of a Battle Area Clearance Unit who were tasked with the removal of mines and unexploded ordnance from the beaches and surrounding area. When Coastal Artillery was disbanded in 1956 all the guns were taken away and scrapped.

Military Museum.

The River Ouse is a 35 mile (56 km) long river that flows through West and East Sussex that you can walk beside on walk 5. It rises near Lower Beeding in West Sussex and flows eastwards and then southwards to reach the sea at Newhaven. The river forms the main spine of an extensive network of smaller streams of which the River Uck is the main tributary. As it nears the coast it passes through Lewes and Laughton Levels which is an area of flat low-lying land that borders the river and another tributary, the Glynde Reach. At the time of the Domesday Book in 1086 it was a large tidal inlet but over the following centuries some attempts were made to reclaim some of the valley floor for agriculture by building embankments. However, drainage was hampered by the build-up of a large shingle bar which formed across the mouth of the river by longshore drift (a geological process that consists of the transportation of sediments such as clay, silt, pebbles, sand or shingle along the coast parallel to the shoreline, which is dependent on the angle of incoming wave direction).

On the lower river, Newhaven became an important port and barge traffic continued using the river up as far as Lewes until the 1950s. The river provides habitat for many varieties of fish, including unusually large sea trout that swim up-river to spawn in the higher tributaries. There are also populations of pike and carp both of which can exceed 30 pounds (14 kg) in weight. Other species include barbel, roach, rudd, perch, chub, bream and tench; rarer breeds include grayling, stone loach, river lampreys and bullheads. The tidal stretches contain fish that can tolerate the lower levels of salt found in brackish water and include flounder, grey mullet, bass, twait shad and sea lampreys.

Lewes Brooks is a Site of Special Scientific Interest on the Levels to the west of the river below Lewes covering an area of 822.8 acres (333 ha). It is noted for its wide diversity of water beetles, rare snails, flies and moths. The habitat is enhanced by a graduation in the water which varies from fresh in the west to brackish in the east. Walkers can follow the course of the river by using the Sussex Ouse Valley Way, a 42 mile long distance footpath.

PIDDINGHOE

Piddinghoe is a village in the Lewes District of East Sussex, located in the valley of the River Ouse between Lewes and Newhaven. Piddinghoe will be visited on walk 5.

The village was once a central player in Sussex smuggling and it is notable for having the only remaining bottle-shaped brick kiln in the country. The kiln is located next to the Lewes Road and the first reference to a brickyard in this location occurs in the 1817 Land Tax registry which gives an indication of the construction date of the original kiln. The brickworks continued until closure in 1913 but although most of the industrial buildings were removed the kiln survived but began to deteriorate until the late 1970s when it was restored. The restoration involved the careful dismantling of the structure and a painstaking rebuild using as many of the original materials as possible.

Bottle-shaped brick kiln.

St John's church is one of three in the Ouse Valley with a round Norman tower, the others being at nearby Southease and Lewes. The church was built in the twelfth century and has a round flint tower; the north arcade dates from the twelfth century and in

Salmon weather vane on St John's church.

the early thirteenth century the chancel, north aisle and south arcade were refashioned. In 1882-4 the church underwent restoration under the direction of Philip Currey, the architect of the Russian Memorial in Lewes. A weathervane in the shape of a salmon can be seen at the top of the tower. Rudyard Kipling's description of it is as a 'gilded dolphin' in his poem 'Sussex' may be indicative of his failing eyesight. The extract reads:

River Ouse at Piddinghoe.

> I will go north about the shaws
> And the deep ghylls that breed
> Huge oaks and old, the which we hold
> No more than Sussex weed;
> Or south where windy Piddinghoe's
> Begilded dolphin veers
> And red beside wide-bankèd Ouse
> Lie down our Sussex steers.

An old saying of unknown origin says that 'Piddinghoe people shoe their magpies'. One theory for this is that it refers to the habit of shoeing oxen, which if black and white, were called magpies.

The village is regularly visited by sailing enthusiasts as the water by the village is a fine location for dinghy sailing and windsurfing.

ENGLISH CHANNEL

Whilst walking along the East Sussex coast you are never far from the English Channel. If you follow the book from Brighton to Camber Sands it is on your right-hand side all the way. So, I thought I would take this opportunity to give you some facts and figures about it.

The English Channel, also known as the Channel, is considered by many people merely to be the stretch of water that separates the south of England from northern France and that to get between the two you go by ferry or the Channel Tunnel; it is, of course, much more than this. The English Channel (from here referred to as the Channel) is an arm of the Atlantic Ocean that links to the southern part of the North Sea by the Strait of Dover at its north-eastern end and it is the busiest shipping area in the world.

It is approximately 350 miles long (560 km) and its width varies from 150 miles (240 km) to 21 miles (34 km) in the Strait of Dover in Kent and covers an area of 29,000 sq. miles (75,000 sq. km). The Strait of Dover, at the eastern end, is the narrowest point and its widest point is near its midpoint between Lyme Bay and the Gulf of Saint Malo. It is quite shallow with an average depth of 390 ft (120m) at its widest part to 148 ft (45m) between Dover and Calais.

Pleasure boat on the English Channel.

Between the Isle of Wight and the mainland there is a small parallel strait known as the Solent which is 20 miles (32km) long and varies between 2.5 and 5 miles (4 and 8 km) in width. The Solent is a major shipping lane for passenger, freight and military vessels and is an important area for water sports particularly yachting hosting the famous yearly Cowes Week.

Newhaven-Dieppe ferry.

Until the eighteenth century it was known colloquially to the English as the "Narrow Sea" and it was never defined as a political border or considered the property of a nation. The name "English Channel" has been widely used since the early eighteenth century, possibly originating from the designation "Engelse Kanaal" on Dutch sea maps from the sixteenth century onwards. The French have used the name La Manche since the seventeenth century; the name is said to refer to the Channel's sleeve shape (la manche is French for sleeve).

There are several major islands in the Channel, the most notable being the Isle of Wight. The other main islands are the Channel Islands which are British Crown dependencies off the coast of France.

The Channel acts as a funnel that amplifies the tidal range and in the U.K. Shipping Forecast the Channel is divided into the following areas, from the east: Dover, Wight, Portland, Plymouth.

Pleasure boat on the English Channel.

The Channel has traffic on both the UK-Europe and North Sea-Atlantic routes, and is the world's busiest seaway with over 500 ships per day. After an accident in January 1971 and a series of collisions with wreckage in February, the Dover TSS, the world's first radar-controlled Traffic Separation Scheme was set up by the International Maritime Organisation. The scheme means that vessels travelling north must use the French side of the Channel and vessels travelling south must use the English side; there is a separation zone between the two lanes. In December 2002 the Norwegian-flagged MV *Tricolor*, that was carrying £30m of luxury cars, sank 20 miles (32 km) northwest of Dunkirk after it collided with the container ship *Kariba* in fog. The cargo ship *Nicola* ran into the wreckage the next day; there was no loss of life.

The shore-based long-range traffic control system was updated in 2003 and there is a series of traffic separation systems in operation. Although the system is unable to reach the levels of safety obtained from aviation systems such as the Traffic Collision Avoidance System (TCAS) it has reduced the number of shipping accidents.

Rampion is an offshore wind farm development by E.ON, off the Sussex coast. It is located between 8 and 16 miles (13 and 25 km) from the shore and is situated off the coastal towns of Worthing to the west, Brighton in the centre and Seaford to the east. It lies in an irregular elongated area, approximately 17 miles (28 km) in an east to west direction and approximately 6.2 miles (10 km) in a north to south direction, and covers 27.8 sq. miles (72 sq. km).

Commissioned in April 2018, the area has become a local landmark and can be seen from great distances but its appearance generates mixed opinions. Rampion Offshore Wind Farm is now generating enough green electricity to power the equivalent of around 350,000 UK homes; this is around half of the homes in Sussex. It was in July 2010 that the public voted for the name Rampion following a schools' competition. Rampion is the county flower of Sussex and the name was submitted by Davison High School.

The farm comprises:

WIND TURBINES
Number of turbines - 116
Installed capacity 400MW
Rating per turbine 3.45MW
Turbine height to hub 80m
Turbine height to blade tip 140m
Length of blades 55m
Diameter of blades 112m

CABLES
Buried onshore cables 27km
Inter-array cables (total) 144km
Array cable strings each with nine to ten turbines 12
Array cable voltage 33kv
Length off offshore export cables 16km
Onshore cable voltage 150 kV circuits

FOUNDATIONS
Monopile foundations 116
Foundation weight 550-800 tonnes
Foundation length 60-80m
Transition piece weight 250 tonnes

OFFSHORE SUBSTATION
Offshore substation 1
Offshore substation weight 3000 tonnes
Offshore substation converts power to 150 kV
Onshore substation converts power to 400 kV
Substation jacket foundation weight 900 tonnes

PROJECT BENEFITS
Annual power generation 1,400 GWh
UK homes supplied equivalent (approx..) 350,000
Approx. emission reductions per annum 6000,000 tonnes

PLEASE NOTE: At the time of writing this book plans for Rampion 2 had been submitted for consideration, and are still awaiting a decision. The plans would be an expansion of the existing Rampion 1 site and the proposed project has the potential to help meet the UK's climate change mitigation goals and government targets for offshore wind generation. If approved, the specifications listed would be out of date but can still be used to make comparisons; for example, they are assessing a maximum height of a 325m tip height which is 2.3 times the height of the existing Rampion turbines. Greater blade 'tip heights' have been the key to advances in technology to date and the power of offshore turbines has increased 5-fold in just twenty years. The maximum number of turbines for Rampion 2 will be 116, the same as Rampion 1 and will not be any closer to the shore than the existing turbines. It is hoped that Rampion 2 will be operational by the end of the decade.

Each year many travellers cross beneath the Channel using the Channel Tunnel. A tunnel was first proposed in the early nineteenth century and the tunnel finally opened in 1994, connecting the UK and France by rail. Today it is a routine journey to travel between Paris or Brussels and London on the Eurostar train. Freight trains also use the tunnel and cars, coaches and lorries are carried on Eurostar Shuttle trains between Folkestone and Calais.

Coastal resorts on both sides of the Channel, such as Brighton and Deauville, started an era of aristocratic tourism in the early nineteenth century, which developed into the seaside tourism that has shaped resorts around the world. Short trips across the Channel for leisure purposes are often referred to as Channel Hopping, or as I know it, Booze Cruise.

Now you can do walk 5 which starts along the River Ouse to reach the fish on Piddinghoe church before returning to Newhaven Fort. Our next stop is Seaford where we visit the old Tide Mills, Martello Tower No. 74 and the much-photographed coastguards cottages set against a backdrop of the Seven Sisters cliffs.

Rampion Wind Farm through the sea haze.

SUGGESTED WALK

WALK 5. Newhaven Harbour and Fort, River Ouse and Piddinghoe (8.75 miles 14.1 km)

Parking. Park in Lower Place North Car Park off Essex Place (nearby Post code BN9 9DT). Although this is a long walk it is not that difficult. It starts with a long walk beside the River Ouse to Piddinghoe church before following a concrete track that climbs gradually (steeply in a couple of short stretches) to Peacehaven before walking across mildly undulating fields and cliff edges to reach Newhaven Fort; there is only one stile. Refreshments are available at Newhaven at the start/finish and at Newhaven Fort Tea Room.

1. From the entrance to the car park go right down Essex Place which is signed as a T-Junction. At the end of the car park go immediately right and go under the road (North Way). On the far side turn left along a wide path and in 25 yards go right along a narrow concrete path with a green metal fence on your right. At the end go left and follow the road and when it curves left go right down a concrete path for 15 yards to reach a 2-way footpath sign. Go right and follow the path which soon becomes a grassy path beside the River Ouse. (If you are wondering, the impressive looking silver building on the other side of the river is the Newhaven Waste Incinerator. The facility treats household waste that cannot be reused, composted or recycled and generates electricity from it that is sold to the National Grid and is enough to supply 25,000 homes.)

River Ouse by Newhaven Waste Incinerator.

Piddinghoe Lake.

As the river curves left you will see the top of Piddinghoe church with its salmon-shaped weather vane which you will be visiting shortly. Pass Piddinghoe Lake on your left which is popular with anglers, go through two gates and immediately after passing a distinctive brick building go left by a sign saying 'Footpath Only'. Walk up to reach a small parking area with St John's church on your right with its salmon (is it upside down?).

Salmon on St John's.

Village sign.

2. Continue to the left of the church to reach a minor road by the Piddinghoe Village sign, which also has a fish, and continue right to reach Lewes Road. Go right for about 30 yards then cross over and go up an access road which is Harping Hill (there is a 2-way footpath sign in the right-hand hedgerow). Now we are going to follow this road, climbing fairly steeply in a couple of places but soon enjoying panoramic views including the Rampion Offshore Wind Farm. (As you look over to your left you will see a mast which is fairly close to Newhaven Fort and that is where you will be near the end of your walk.) Follow the road, ignoring any footpaths to the right and cross a stile which is to the left of a wide gate that goes across the road. Just continue with Peacehaven in view ahead and at a junction with a 3-way signpost (2 bridleway / 1 footpath) go left along a wide access track.

Follow the track around to the left with hedgerow on your left and then continue across open fields. On the far side of this field go right by electricity lines and follow the left field edge with hedgerow on your left again aiming for Peacehaven. In about 100 yards go left down a grassy path with a wire fence on your right. Follow the path down, then up, then pass to the rear of houses on your right. Go right at a parking area and in 15 yards go left along a gravelled access road, Cornwall Avenue, not signed.

3. At the end you reach a road. Go left for 20 yards then go right down Searle Avenue. At the end you reach Coast Road, go left for 20 yards then go right down Seaview Road. At the end go left along The Promenade then continue along the cliff edge path. (Optional detour – there is an access point here where you can go down steps to reach the path at the bottom of the cliffs but unfortunately the path does not go very far.)

View from cliff edge path.

Just follow the cliff edge path (keeping children away from the edge), cross a wooden bridge and continue now aiming for the Coastguard Tower and West Pier (you can see the mast that I mentioned earlier over to your left). Pass Newhaven Heights holiday homes on your left then reaching a sign for Castle Hill Nature Reserve. 25 yards past this sign go left at a ground-level footpath sign and follow the path up and around to go past the front of the Coastguard Tower.

Cliffs from bottom of steps. View from cliff edge path.

Continue past the tower then take the path that goes slightly inland to reach an access road. Go right down the road and in about 30 yards go right along a gravelled path to reach the car park at Newhaven Fort. Go through the car park and the Fort entrance is at the far end. (Explore the Fort and from

Coastguard Tower.

Newhaven Fort.

42

Military Museum.

high up by the gun that overlooks the sea look back at the River Ouse and East to see Tide Mills and Seaford Head in the distance that you will be exploring in the next chapter.)

4. From the Fort entrance go ahead down the road directly opposite and then continue along the next road using the right-hand pavement with Newhaven Marina Boat Park on your right. At a mini roundabout go right along West Quay and in about 120 yards go right along the path that takes you beside the River Ouse soon passing a Lifeboat Station. Just follow this path passing numerous fresh fish outlets until you reach a major road junction. Cross over at the nearest set of traffic lights and go straight ahead up Bridge Street. At the end go left by The Ship pub and in 20 yards go right along St Luke's Lane back to the car park.

CHAPTER 4
TIDE MILLS & SEAFORD

TIDE MILLS

Tide Mills is a derelict village 1.2 miles (2 km) south-east of Newhaven and 2.5 miles (4 km) north-west of Seaford but it is on the Seaford side of the River Ouse – and is visited on walk 6. The village was condemned in 1936 and abandoned in 1939.

Thomas Pelham, the politician and prime minister, who also held the title Duke of Newcastle, owned land at Bishopstone and obtained an Act of Parliament which allowed him to use the foreshore of this land for the site of a tide mill (a water mill driven by tidal rise and fall). Construction began in 1761 but Pelham died in 1768 before its completion in 1788. Three years later, it was advertised for sale in the *Sussex Weekly Advertiser* and at that time it contained five pairs of mill stones, which could produce 130 quarters (1.65 tonnes) of wheat each week. However, the location was a problem and in 1792 large quantities of flour and wheat were destroyed when the site was hit by a violent storm.

Thomas Barton bought the mill site and made a series of improvements to make the mill more efficient. He built a new three-storey mill building to house 16 pairs of stones, which produced up to 1500 sacks (190 tonnes) of flour per week. Ownerships changed as a series of partnerships were created and then dissolved. Barton was in partnership with Edmund Catt just prior to 1800 but by 1801 that agreement was no longer in place. Catt then entered into an agreement with his cousin William Catt, but William dissolved this in 1807. William Catt was part of a family who had many farming and milling interests and he was a keen businessman. He managed the mill well and it became very profitable despite the occasional storm damage, such as the storm of 1820 which damaged the building and washed away some of the mill dam.

Tide Mills ruins.

The census of 1851 showed that there were 60 men working at the mill and most of them lived in cottages which Catt had built around the site. He also built a school and although the conditions were quite basic a thriving community developed and the workers appreciated the facilities provided for their families at a time when such provisions were rare. After the railway line from Newhaven to Seaford was opened a siding was constructed which ran between the cottages, enabling large quantities of flour to be transported to Newhaven from where much of it was shipped to London by sea.

The mill closed in 1883 and was used as bonded warehouses until it was pulled down in 1901 and the village condemned as unfit for habitation in 1936 with the last residents removed in 1939.

Railway siding through Tide Mills.

SEAFORD

Seaford is a town on the south coast that was one of the main ports serving southern England during the Middle Ages but its fortunes declined due to coastal sedimentation silting up its harbour and persistent raids by French pirates.

The coastal confederation of Cinque Ports in the medieval period consisted of forty-two towns and villages and Seaford was included under the "Limb" of Hastings. Between 1350 and 1550, the French burned down the town several times.

In the sixteenth and seventeenth centuries the people of Seaford were known as "cormorants" or "shags" because they were known for looting ships that had been wrecked in the bay and local legend has it that the residents would occasionally cause ships to run aground by placing fake harbour lights on the cliffs. One cold December night in 1815 a copper-bottomed ship called *The Adamant* sank in Seaford Bay. The ship which had previously been a gun-boat called the *Thrasher* was sailing from Malta to London with a full cargo of wine, almonds, oil, quicksilver (mercury), Turkish carpets, books, linen, cumin seeds, feathers, skins, gall-nuts (used for medicine), lace, opium and sulphur. The ship had struck rocks off Seaford Head cliffs during a storm. The pilot and other boats from Newhaven Harbour managed to pull her away from the rocks but she sank nearby; luckily the crew was able to take to these boats and there was no loss of life.

It was said that the people of Seaford slept with their doors open during bad weather so that they didn't miss the unexpected bounty of a shipwreck as these 'Seaford Shags' considered that goods of a wrecked ship were rightfully theirs. The authorities only managed to salvage 40 of the 60 barrels of wine and although over the next few weeks some items were recovered from various dubious sources the 'Seaford Shags' presumably had a good Christmas.

Seaford's fortunes were revived in the nineteenth century with the arrival of the railway connecting the town to Lewes and London, and Seaford became a small seaside resort town and more recently a commuter town for the larger settlements of Eastbourne and Brighton as well as London.

The town lies on the coast near Seaford Head roughly mid-way between the mouths of the River Ouse (described in Chapter 3) and the River Cuckmere (described in Chapter 6). To the north the town faces the South Downs and this stretch of coast is designated for its

Splash Point.

Seaford Head at Splash Point.

View of Seaford from Seaford Head.

geological and ecological features as Seaford to Beachy Head Site of Special Scientific Interest.

Seaford used to have excellent beaches which were supplied with sand by longshore drift moving the sand along the coast from west to east but in the early twentieth century a large breakwater was built at Newhaven Harbour and the harbour entrance was regularly dredged. These works cut off the supply of fresh sand and by the 1980s the beach had all but vanished with the shoreline becoming steep, narrow and stony. However, this made Seaford an area attractive for water-sports enthusiasts as the water visibility was good and there was a rapid drop-off into deep water although it discouraged more general seaside visitors. So, in 1987 a major beach recharge project was completed which used shingle dredged from the seabed off the Isle of Wight. Today Seaford's beach is very popular and enjoys sea temperatures up to 20° Celsius (68 °F). To the east of Seaford, below the chalk cliffs, is a beach called Hope Gap and it was the location for a film called *Hope Gap* with stars including Annette Bening, Bill Nighy and Josh O'Connor.

Seaford Head is a 150.2 hectare (371 acre) Local Nature Reserve east of Seaford that is part of the Seaford to Beachy Head Site of Special Scientific Interest. An area of 83 hectares (210 acres) is owned by the Seaford Town Council and managed by the Sussex Wildlife Trust and the remainder is divided between the Seven Sisters County Park and the National Trust. The site has diverse habitats with chalk grassland, chalk cliffs, scrub, vegetated shingle, wet grassland, saltmarsh and rockpools. Grassland flora includes kidney vetch, squinancywort, moon carrot and clustered bellflower and there are butterflies including silver-spotted skipper, chalkhill blue and Adonis blue.

The 18th hole on Seaford Head Golf Course is 300ft (91.4m) above sea level with a drop of 150ft (45.7m) to the fairway below and golfers from all over the world travel to play it.

The Coastguard Cottages with the backdrop of the Seven Sisters cliffs are one of the most iconic views in East Sussex as well as the UK. It is one of the most visited sites and most photographed and has been used in several TV programmes. The cottages (passed on walk 6) were built soon after the National Coastguard Service was founded in 1822; prior to this Cuckmere Haven was an important place for smuggling. Since then, the cliff face in front of the cottages has retreated by more than 30 metres due to coastal erosion and this combined with the loss of shingle from the beach below due to wave action has put the cottages in danger.

Coastguard Cottages and the Seven Sisters.

Seaford's Martello Tower is located at the far eastern end of Seaford seafront. It is No. 74 of an original 103 small defensive forts and it is the first of several towers that we will visit in this book. The towers were part of defences built when Napoleon threatened to cross the 'ditch' (English Channel) in 1803. They were built from Aldeburgh in Suffolk around the coast to Eastbourne; the one in Seaford was built as an after-thought when it was realised that there were not enough defences for Newhaven and Tide Mills.

The towers were based on the design of a tower on the island of Corsica as noted by Admiral Jervis, commanding HMS *Victory*, when he attempted to recapture it for loyalist islanders from French rebels. The tower was on Mortella Point, so called because of myrtle bushes growing there and this name became corrupted by the British to Martello. The land in Seaford was purchased in 1806 and the tower built between then and 1810 at a cost of £18,000 using half a million bricks. Two other towers which would have provided covering fire were planned but never built so this was the last tower in the chain, although many others were built worldwide.

A waterproof brick 'dry moat' was made before the construction of the tower could start as it was below sea level. This had a central slate-lined cistern to receive rain water through pipes built into the walls from the roof. Above this a three-storey tower consisted of a storage area and gunpowder magazine at moat level, a living area for an officer and 24 men at ground level and the roof housed the 24-pounder cannon, now replaced by a 32-pounder. Access to the tower would have been via a drawbridge on the landward side but this was destroyed when the cannon fell on it while being moved by John Lee in 1880.

Martello Tower No. 74 (Seaford Museum).

The design of these small round defensive forts followed a standard plan although they varied in size. A typical South East Martello would be about 13.7m in diameter at its base and up to 12m tall. The masonry walls were built of brick and were up to 2.5m thick. Inside there were two main floors, the lower floor housing supplies and powder store and the first floor the men's and officer's quarters. A single Martello housed between 15 and 25 men; a garrison of up to 24 men and one officer. The flat roof would be equipped with one or more cannon capable of rotating through 360 degrees and the entrance would be about 3 metres above ground level, reachable by a retractable ladder.

Nicknamed the Tardis by its visitors the tower is now a museum run by the Seaford Museum & Heritage Society and inside there is a deceptive 5000 square feet of display area which includes the roof with cannon, entrance floor with museum shop, the lower floor of the tower and the covered dry moat area.

Now you can do the associated walk which starts by the Tide Mill ruins then visits Martello Tower No. 74 and the iconic view of the coastguard cottages with the Seven Sisters cliffs behind. I will see you slightly inland for the next chapter when we explore Sussex's two hill figures; the White Horse at Litlington and the Long Man of Wilmington.

Cannon with 360-degree rotation.

SUGGESTED WALK

WALK 6. Tide Mill ruins, Martello Tower & Coastguard Cottages
(10.25 miles 16.5 km)

Parking. There is free parking in the car park at the start of Mill Drove which is right next to the A259. This is a long walk but most of it is on a there-and-back route along level ground along the seafront. Midway (or end) there is a long but mainly steady climb up on to Seaford Head for views across to the Seven Sisters by the Coastguard Cottages, there are a couple of short but steep climbs here as well but there are no stiles. Refreshments are available from various beachfront kiosks.

PLEASE NOTE this walk can be reduced to 5.5 miles (8.8 km) by doing it as a point-to-point walk and having a second car parked at South Hill Barn Car Park, Chyngton Way, BN25 4JQ; this is a free car park but please check. You will still see all of the points of interest except a close up of the Air Navigation Point.

1. From the height restriction at the car park entrance go left along the access road, cross a railway line and continue to reach Tide Mills derelict village. Walk through the ruins to reach the beach. (Newhaven Fort is on the hill to your right and Newhaven West Pier with lighthouse can also be seen.)

Newhaven Fort taken from Mill Creek.

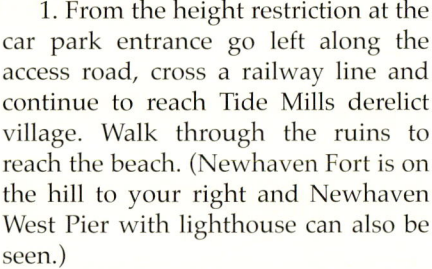

Tide Mills ruins.

Lighthouse on West Pier.

Go left along the concrete/pebble path looking out for the remains of the railway siding which ran through the village. Just keep going as you are ultimately aiming to be on the top of Seaford Head (cliff) ahead. Just after Tide Mills you pass the popular Newhaven & Seaford Sailing Club and when the path runs beside the road you have reached the start of the main area of Seaford. Soon you reach Martello Tower No. 74. It is the first of ten Martello Towers passed in this book and it is the only one that is accessible as it serves as a museum; the others are private or derelict. I would strongly urge you to visit this one as the museum is crammed with interesting artefacts and once inside try to understand the construction and design of the tower; for example, look out for the small area which gives you an idea of how thick the walls are. (My thanks to Phil who gave me a guided tour of the tower, even though it was closed, so that I could get the photos for this book.) From the tower walk to the right of some colourful beach huts and soon when the path ends you have reached Splash Point at the start of Seaford Head. Explore this area being mindful of the risk of falling rocks off the cliffs.

Martello Tower No. 74 (Seaford Museum).

Aiming at enemy French ships c1810.

2. Where the path ended go to the left and climb up the path, signposted 'Vanguard Way', go up steps and follow the path by the cliff edge climbing up to its highest point and soon you find yourself beside the famous 18th hole on the golf course. Without disturbing any players look at the hole. It is 300ft (91.4m) above sea level with a drop of 150ft (45.7m) to the fairway below and golfers from all over the world have travelled to play it. (When standing on the 489-yard Par 5 hole you are aiming for the flag which is way down by the houses in front of you.) Just past the 18th hole you get a view of the Air Navigation Point, which you can get a close-up of if you are doing the full walk, over to your left (it is a type of short-range radio navigation system for aircraft, enabling aircraft with a receiving unit to find its position and stay on course by receiving radio signals transmitted by a network of fixed ground radio beacons).

18th hole – 150ft down to fairway.

View to Seven Sisters.

From this point you enter the Seaford Head Local Nature Reserve and you continue with fine views of the Seven Sisters (which you will walk on walk 9) and in the far distance you can see Belle Tout lighthouse (which you will pass on walk 10). Go through a gate and descend with lovely views ahead, then curve slightly left and climb steeply up again. The path

Coastguard Cottages by cliff edge.

continues to curve to the left and soon you reach the Coastguard Cottages with the famous views across to the Seven Sisters. This area has been used in many TV programmes and is one of the most photographed scenes in Britain – I hope you have picked a sunny day.

3. From the Coastguard Cottages go left up the wide stony track and just follow it climbing gently. At a crossing of paths continue ahead to reach South Hill Barn car park where you can end the walk if you have parked a second car here. Go left and follow the wide concrete access road with a wire fence on your left. When the fence ends go immediately left and follow the path with the fence on your left (NOTE: if you wanted to get a close-up view of the Air Navigation Tower continue along the concrete access road for another 25 yards then go left along a side path to reach it.)

Air Navigation.

4. At the end of the fence, on the far side, go right and start your return journey along the same route. Follow the cliff edge path off Seaford Head, re-pass the Martello Tower and maybe visit it if you didn't on your outward journey, then continue along the seafront back to Tide Mills. (As you go keep a lookout for the Transmanche Ferries using Newhaven Harbour and if you want you can divert over to your right to explore the shops, bars and restaurants at Seaford which are a little way back from the seafront.) At Tide Mills go right by a 3-way footpath sign and follow the concrete path back over the railway line and ahead to reach the car park.

CHAPTER 5
LITLINGTON & WILMINGTON

LITLINGTON

Litlington is a very lightly populated village in the Cuckmere Valley located 3 miles (4.8 km) from Seaford. The name is Saxon and literally means Litl's (followers or possibly family's) homestead; it is also possibly a corruption of Littleton but there is no evidence for it missing its -ing component.

The village is small and like the rest of the parish, which extends to take in much of the Seven Sisters Country Park, is on the left bank of a narrow valley in the signature narrow band of the South Downs National Park.

St Michael the Archangel's church is a very good example of a Downland church which is built of flint with stone dressings and a white painted weather-boarded wooden belfry tower which supports a broach spire covered with wooden shingles. The main part of the building is thought to have been built around 1150 but there are windows in the chancel which may well be Norman.

Litlington Tea Garden is an historic tea garden nestled in the rolling hills of the Cuckmere Valley. It was established in the Victorian period over 150 years ago and became very popular with the advent of the motor car, when people would drive out at the weekends from towns like London and Brighton.

Friston Forest.

St Michael the Archangel's church.

Friston Forest lies within the South Downs National Park between Lullington Heath National Nature Reserve and the Seven Sisters Country Park and it is the largest area of recently established forest in south-east England. The expansive beech woodland is ideal for those who love exploring woodland and has walking and cycling trails as well as great views of the Cuckmere River and the South Downs.

Litlington White Horse.   Cuckmere River.

The Litlington White Horse is a chalk hill figure depicting a horse situated on Hindover Hill, known locally as High-and-Over, in the South Downs overlooking the Cuckmere River to the west of Litlington. The current horse was cut in 1924 by John T. Ade, Mr Bovis and Eric Hobbis in a single night and is 93 ft long and 65 ft high and contains 6 tons of chalk; a previous horse existed on this site. The horse is owned by the National Trust who regularly clean and maintain it along with local volunteers. The Litlington White Horse is one of two hill figures in East Sussex the other being the Long Man of Wilmington which is 3 miles away.

The origin and date for the original White Horse is uncertain. One view is that it was created by James Pagden of Frog Firle Farm with his two brothers and cousin William Ade in 1838 to commemorate the coronation of Queen Victoria. Another view is that it was cut in 1860 by two local boys who had noticed that a patch of bare chalk resembled a horse's head and so they cut away the rest of the horse to complete it. Although the first story is the most likely, it is possible that the boys recut the horse after it had been neglected, thus leading to this confusion.

The current horse was carved by John T. Ade (who was the son of the original horse's creator William Ade), Mr Bovis and Eric Hobbis in one night on the full moon of 20 February 1924. Originally designed by John Ade in the winter of 1923 he drew inspiration from the Westbury White Horse on the Salisbury Plain in Wiltshire. Based on Ade's letters they first laid out the horse using ropes and pegs at Ade's farm in preparation for its cutting at Litlington. During the February full moon, the men cut the horse using a 'stick' of 35 inches as a measurement for a quick transfer of their design. It was cut without the knowledge of the residents who awoke startled by the horse's appearance on the side of the hill; this may have been the motivation behind the speedy cutting.

During the 1930s the horse was covered by the ministry of defence to stop it being used as a location marker for the Luftwaffe in WWII. The rushed uncovering of the horse in 1945 by contractors from the Ministry of Defence resulted in several changes to the horse's original shape, including only one front leg being recut. This was not corrected until the full moon of the 9-10 June 1949, when between

10pm and 3 am, John T. Ade with Bovis and Hobbis made several further changes to the horse's original appearance, including recutting an additional front leg and readjusting its back which 'had shifted uphill a bit from saddle to rump'.

In the late 1980s, East Sussex County Council cleaned (scoured) the horse and installed wooden boards around the horse to keep the chalk in place, they also installed a perimeter fence to prevent damage being caused by livestock. In 1991, Frog Firle Farm and the White Horse were acquired by the National Trust who have since maintained the horse, the figure being last scoured in 2016. In May 2017 the horse was vandalised with the adding of a unicorn horn which was quickly removed.

Litlington White Horse.

White Horse Folklore:

Local folklore suggests that the horse was originally cut as a memorial to a local girl whose horse bolted when riding along the brow of Hindover Hill, throwing her down the hill which resulted in her death.

Another story suggests that the figure originally depicted a dog which was cut by a grieving boy to mark the grave of his dog that was killed alongside or in the River Cuckmere below. Supposedly, due to erosion of the dog's nose and legs over the following years it began to look like a horse, causing the figure to take its present form. There is no evidence to support either of these stories.

WILMINGTON

The Long Man of Wilmington, also known as Wilmington Giant, is a hill figure on the steep slopes of Windover Hill near Wilmington. The figure is 235 ft (72m) tall, holds two staves and is designed to look in proportion when viewed from below; locally it was once often called the 'Green Man'.

The guardian of the South Downs has baffled archaeologists and historians for hundreds of years; is it a fertility symbol? ancient warrior? early

The Long Man of Wilmington.

eighteenth century folly? – the true reason for this figure may never be known.

In 1925 the monument was given to the Sussex Archaeological Society by the Duke of Devonshire and they have cared for the scheduled monument ever since and ensured that it remains free for public access.

The Long Man is Europe's largest portrayal of the human form and dates back to at least 1710 when the surveyor John Rowley illustrated the figure. In 1766 the artist William Burrell made a drawing during his visit to Wilmington Priory. Rowley's drawing suggests that the original figure was a shadow or indentation in the grass rather than a solid line and the face had a distinctive helmet shape, giving credence to the idea that he was a war-God.

Wilmington Priory ruins – on private grounds.

Until the nineteenth Century when it was marked out in yellow bricks the image was only visible in certain light conditions. It is claimed that during this restoration the feet were incorrectly positioned; but despite local legend there is no evidence, historical or archaeological, to suggest that prudish Victorians robbed the Giant of his manhood.

During WWII the figure was painted green to prevent enemy aviators using it as a landmark. Restoration work in 1969 replaced the bricks with concrete blocks that are now regularly painted so that the Long Man is visible from miles away.

There are many theories regarding his origin. Some are convinced that he is prehistoric while some others believe that he is the work of an artistic monk from the nearby Priory between the eleventh and fifteenth centuries. Roman coins bearing a similar figure suggest that he existed in the fourth century and there are parallels with a helmeted figure found on Anglo-Saxon ornaments. Until new evidence is unearthed, we will have to content ourselves with the words of Reverend A. A. Evans who said, 'The Giant keeps his secret and from his hillside flings out a perpetual challenge'.

The Long Man is one of two major extant human hill figures in England, the other being the Cerne Abbas Giant, north of Dorchester. The Long Man is also one of two hill figures in East Sussex the other being the Litlington White Horse which is 3 miles south-west of the Long Man and is featured and walked past in this chapter.

The church of St Mary and St Peter is in the village of Wilmington and is passed on walk 8. It was founded in the late eleventh century to serve the villagers in a rural area at the foot of the South Downs and it also functioned as a priory church for the monks from the adjacent Wilmington Priory to which it was physically connected. The building has benefitted from sympathetic restoration over the centuries including a series of works by prominent architects Paley and Austin in the Victorian era and internal renovation after a fire in the early twenty-first century. The church is recorded in the National Heritage List for England as a designated Grade I listed building.

After the Norman Conquest in 1066 monks from Grestain Abbey, a Benedictine monastery in Normandy, took possession of the land around Wilmington. They founded Wilmington Priory to administer their territory and two or three monks lived there. It was never a large community and no separate abbey church was ever built, instead, the monks shared the chancel of the village church. This was in existence by 1100 and served the farmers and villagers of Winelton, as it was known then; the church was connected to the priory by a cloister. In common with other alien priories (religious establishments such as a monastery or convent, which were under the control of another religious house outside England – usually in France) in England, Wilmington Priory was suppressed by King Henry V in 1414 and it fell into ruins. Thereafter the church functioned solely as a parish church.

The thirteenth century north chapel, now a vestry, contains a well-regarded stained-glass window known as the 'Bee and Butterfly Window'. It was badly damaged by the fire and was replaced with a new design which kept the same theme but added images of Saint Peter surrounded by several insects and a phoenix rising from a fire.

The Wilmington Madonna on the north wall of the chancel is a strange figure which was removed from the outside wall in 1948 to a corresponding wall inside the chancel. One theory suggests that the carving is like the gargoyles found outside medieval churches. Although it has certain features common to medieval angels, recent cleaning of the figure suggests it to be an early Norman representation

Bee and Butterfly window.

Wilmington Madonna.

57

of the Madonna as it includes the remnants of what may well be a Christ child on the main figure's knees. An even earlier date for the carving is not improbable and could suggest a connection with some pagan fertility cult. (It is found just before the altar on the left above head height.)

A huge ancient yew tree in the churchyard has been scientifically dated as 1600 years old with a girth of 23ft (7m); some say the yew could be 2000 years old, more than twice as old as the church itself. Beneath the yew is a stone, said to be a Roman stone, which was found at the bottom of the old Vicarage well by the village well-digger; the stone now lies over his grave. The tree had new wooden props fitted in 2019.

The Long Man is seen by some as a guardian of a gateway which makes the church dedication to St Mary and St Peter quite interesting as St Peter is the guardian of the gates of heaven. This Christianisation of themes is quite common, with a particular attribute of a place or date in pre-Christian times being replaced with an affiliation with a saint who has similar properties or attributes.

Now you can do the two associated walks to visit both hill figures and the 1600-year-old yew tree. The walks have been deliberately kept short so that you can do them both on the same day if you wish as they are only a short distance apart. I will see you back at the coast where we visit the almost extinct village of Exceat, then walk beside the Cuckmere River before venturing out across the Seven Sisters.

Church of St Mary & St Peter.

1600-year-old yew tree which needs supporting.

SUGGESTED WALK

WALK 7. Litlington White Horse, Friston Forest and Cuckmere River
(3.75 miles 6.0 km)

Parking. Friston Forest pay and display car park along Litlington Road – park on the LHS. All parking charges go to the upkeep of Friston Forest and its wildlife). There are a few climbs, a couple of which are fairly steep, six stiles (one is high) and over 85 steps down through Friston Forest. There is one short path that can get a little overgrown followed by a very short but steepish bank to go up – both at the end. Refreshments are available from The Plough & Harrow pub or Litlington Tea Rooms.

1. Go left through the car park and 20 yards past the two pay-and-display meters go right and walk uphill, ignoring the path to your left in a few yards. At the top go left by a 2-way footpath sign on the South Downs Way (SDW). Soon you reach a junction by a 2-way footpath sign for the SDW and you continue ahead going down over 85 steps. At the bottom of the steps go

Litlington White Horse.

left still on the SDW. In about 100 yards you reach a 3-way footpath sign and you go right over a stile. Go up the left edge of a field with your first view of the Litlington White Horse away to your left. (The best views of the horse are from a distance.) Just keep going looking out for kestrels that hunt in the surrounding fields.

At a track go ahead through a swing gate and continue ahead along a right field edge with a view of Alfriston church ahead of you. The path descends and curves to the left of a house and goes out to Clapham Lane, not signed. Go left down the lane and turn right along The Street, not signed. Soon you reach the lovely Plough & Harrow pub where you can take refreshments. (The walk continues by going left along the footpath that is immediately after the pub but you can continue for a very short distance to reach The Litlington Tea Rooms and Crystal Store on the right.)

The Plough & Harrow Pub.

2. Turn left along the footpath that is next to the pub and follow it to the

end to reach the bank of the Cuckmere River, now with the White Horse in view. Go left for a few yards then go right over the bridge at Frog Firle. On the far side, go left and follow the bank of the river until you reach the next bridge, New Bridge, where you cross back over the river. (You could have stayed on the other side of the river but if you have children with you, they love crossing bridges.)

Cuckmere River.

Turn right and follow the river and when you cross a stile where the river bends to the right a few yards further on, go immediately left after the stile. Go along the enclosed path which has watercourses on either side and which can get a little overgrown. At the end go through a gate and ahead / right, over a high stile, to arrive back at Litlington Road. (The car park is about 350 yards along the road to the right and some people prefer to walk down the road rather than go up the bank). Opposite is a very short but steepish bank. Go up the bank and in 10 yards go right along the path beneath trees, walking parallel to the road, to arrive back at the car park.

SUGGESTED WALK

WALK 8. The Long Man of Wilmington & 1600-year-old yew tree
(2.25 miles 3.6 km)

Parking. From the A27, go up The Street and about 200 yards past the church there is a free car park on the right with a signpost opposite in the hedgerow indicating parking. (Post Code for church – BN26 5SW or what3words polite.online.output.) This is a short and easy walk with no stiles. There is a gradual climb at the start and a descent down a chalky

Sheep visiting the Long Man.

path which can be a bit slippery when wet. Refreshments are available from the very popular Sussex Ox pub which sell drinks from local breweries.

1. Leave the car park at its main entrance and cross the road to the footpath directly opposite which is signposted to the Long Man. (Remember the Long Man is best viewed and photographed from a distance, the nearer you get the less you can see of him.) Just follow the enclosed path then head up across a field

The Sussex Ox, Milton Street.

and climb steadily up to arrive at the Long Man. Go through a bridle gate and ahead to reach a notice board at the foot of the figure.

2. Turn right and follow the path with a barbed-wire fence on your left and then continue climbing gently with a barbed-wire fence on your right; away to your right is Arlington Reservoir. Go through a gate and immediately turn right down a chalky path aiming for Milton Street ahead; you may be able to make out the Sussex Ox pub particularly if they have their parasols out in the beer garden. Go through a gate and continue to reach a road. Cross the road, go left for 5 yards then go right and follow the path around to the right and down to reach a lane. Go left down the lane to reach the Sussex Ox pub with their beers, lagers and ciders from local brewers.

Wilmington Priory ruins.

Wilmington Village Pound.

3. Turn right at the pub and follow the quiet lane past Back Lane on the right and in a further 10 yards go right at a footpath sign, Cuckmere Pilgrim Path, go up a couple of steps and ahead across the middle of a field aiming for the church of St Mary and St Peter in view ahead. Pass a marker post en-route and from here you have another view of the Long Man on your right. Continue ahead across a second field which soon curves right towards the church.

On the far side you reach a marker post by an access drive, go left for a few yards then go right through a metal gate into the church graveyard. Visit the church to see the famous Bee and Butterfly window and the Wilmington Madonna and you can't miss the 1600-year-old yew tree having to be propped up by the church doorway. Leave the church by its main entrance and go right up the road. Soon you pass the Wilmington Priory ruins which are on private land but you can get a peek through a gate and from the road. Pass the Wilmington Village Pound (pounds were used to house stray livestock which were only released on payment of a fine; pounds used to be common across the country but now only a few remain) before continuing along the lane back to the car park.

CHAPTER 6
EXCEAT, CUCKMERE HAVEN & THE SEVEN SISTERS

EXCEAT

Exceat (pronounced ex-seat) was a bustling fishing village that was founded in Saxon times. It was sheltered from the weather by the protection of the Cuckmere Valley and some historians believe that it could have been a very successful fishing base. The village was also thought to have been one of the most important naval bases for King Alfred the Great who was widely recognised as the first King of England. Alfred was thought to have had a palace at nearby West Dean and Exceat would have served as one of his main naval bases in his wars against the Danish.

However, the village's glory days would be cut short in the fourteenth century as along with Europe, England suffered heavily when the Black Death arrived in 1347. It was the deadliest pandemic in human history with some estimates suggesting that it wiped out as much as 60 per cent of Europe's population. Exceat was one of the many casualties and in just a few years the population of the village was all but wiped out as, being a port village, Exceat was especially vulnerable to a

Stone memorial for Exceat church.

disease which arrived by boat. To make matters worse, the village began to fall victim to attacks from French raiders who targeted villages on the English coast. The few survivors soon left for pastures new and the village was completely abandoned by the mid 1400s.

Exceat does not now exist except as the Seven Sisters Country Park Visitors Centre and the bridge bears its name. Exceat had a church that once stood high up on the Downs with views over the River Cuckmere; nothing remains of the church but there is a stone marker acting as a memorial to the church and Exceat.

During the 1100s Exceat was one of the most important villages in East Sussex, paying more in taxes than Lewes or Seaford at that time. The village was visited by King Edward I in 1305, which shows the historical importance of Exceat right up to the time it was ravaged by the plague.

CUCKMERE HAVEN

Cuckmere Haven, also known as the Cuckmere estuary, is an area of flood plains where the River Cuckmere meets the English Channel between Eastbourne and Seaford. The river is an ideal example of a meandering river and it contains several oxbow lakes (a U-shaped lake that forms when a wide meander of a river is cut off, creating a free-standing body of water). It is a very popular destination with over 350,000 visitors per year who can enjoy long walks or water activities on the river. The beach at Cuckmere Haven is next to the beautiful and famous chalk cliffs called the Seven Sisters.

The wreck of the *Polynesia*, a German sailing ship that ran aground in April 1890 west of Beachy Head laden with a cargo of sodium nitrate, is exposed at low tide. The beach was also commonly used by smugglers in the sixteenth to eighteenth centuries; for example, in 1783 two gangs of smugglers (each numbering 200 or 300) overcame officers of the law by weight of numbers and carried away a large quantity of goods.

During WWII the site was studied by the Luftwaffe as they flew missions to identify possible landing sites for the invasion of the UK mainland and as a result, the British built a series of counter-landing defences, of which numerous pillboxes, anti-tank obstacles, ditches and tank traps survive. Cuckmere Haven featured heavily in the war effort and at night lights were placed to confuse bombers into thinking they were above Newhaven and an airfield was set up further inland. In addition to the permanent land-based constructions the river was heavily mined.

The East Sussex Transport and Trading Company extracted gravel from the beach at Cuckmere Haven and transported the material to the road at Exceat on a 2-foot (610mm) gauge tramway a mile (1.6 km) long, established in the early 1930s and closed in 1964. The tramway began at the car park on the south side of the main road and the footpath on the east of the river now follows the line of the tramway.

River Cuckmere.

The famous Coastguard Cottages on the western side of the river were described in Chapter 4 and they were passed on the suggested Seaford walk.

Cuckmere Haven is home to a large variety of wildlife and has a rich ecosystem. Sheep and cattle can be seen grazing, keeping the fields at a constant vegetation level. Woodpigeons and rooks pick at the stubble and aquatic birds such as oystercatchers forage in the water meadows; the result is a fertile area of land providing various habitats. The beaches are shingle and there are exposed rockpools along the shoreline at low tide. From 2019 the entire coastline of the South Downs National Park was designated as a Marine Conservation Zone.

The River Cuckmere rises near Henfield, East Sussex, on the southern slopes of the Weald (an area between the parallel chalk escarpments of the North and South Downs). The name of the river may come from an Old English word meaning 'fast-flowing' as it descends over 100m (328 ft) in its first four miles (6.4 km). It flows into the English Channel at Cuckmere Haven and has the only undeveloped river mouth on the Sussex coast. The river has many tributaries at its upper end the principal one being the River Bull; and its main channel begins at Hellingly. After crossing the Low Weald area of farmland, it cuts through the South Downs in its own valley until it reaches the English Channel at Cuckmere Haven between Seaford and the Seven Sisters cliff face. The lower part of its course in the floodplain is marked by meandering (one of a series of regular sinuous curves, bends, loops, turns or windings in a watercourse). The Cuckmere Valley Nature Reserve is located in the lower estuary portion of the river.

Cuckmere Haven.

THE SEVEN SISTERS

The Seven Sisters is a series of chalk cliffs by the English Channel that form part of the South Downs between Seaford and Eastbourne. They are within the South Downs National Park which is bounded by the coast, the River Cuckmere and the A259 road. They are remnants of dry valleys in the chalk South Downs, which are gradually being eroded by the sea. The Seven Sisters Country Park is made up of 280 hectares of chalk cliffs, meandering river valley and open chalk grassland. Starting at Cuckmere Haven the Seven Sisters (cliffs) are named as follows going east to Birling Gap: Haven Brow, Short Brow, Rough Brow, Brass Point, Flagstaff Brow, Flat Hill, Baily's Hill and Went Hill.

As you may have noticed from the list, the Seven Sisters are eight? Cliff erosion has caused an eighth sister to appear which has been named Flagstaff Brow but they are still collectively known as the Seven Sisters.

To the east of the last peak is Birling Gap with the Belle Tout Lighthouse atop the next hill and beyond that is Beachy Head; we will be visiting all of these in Chapter 7 as well as Sherlock Holmes's retirement cottage.

The South Downs Way runs along the cliff edge on its way to its start/end at Eastbourne just a few more miles away. The Seven Sisters cliffs are occasionally used in filmmaking and television productions and can be a stand-in for the more famous White Cliffs of Dover. The Seven Sisters and Beachy Head remain a bright white colour whereas the White Cliffs of Dover are increasingly covered in vegetation and greening as a result. They are featured at the beginning of the film *Robin Hood: Prince of Thieves* and at the end of the film *Atonement* where Robbie and Cecilia always wanted to live. Much of the 2015 feature film *Mr Holmes* was filmed around the Seven Sisters. Starring Ian McKellen as Sherlock Holmes and Laura Linney as his housekeeper Mrs Munro it is set during his retirement in Sussex as the ninety-three-year-old detective struggles to recall the details of his final case because his mind is slowly deteriorating.

The Seven Sisters.

An east-facing photo of the Seven Sisters was included as one of the default landscape wallpapers packaged with Microsoft Windows 7.

Now, if you are feeling adventurous, you can do the associated walk; it is strenuous but rewarding and remember there is no rush. I will see you at East Dean for another cliff walk where we begin at Sherlock Holmes' retirement cottage before passing two lighthouses on our way to Beachy Head.

Seven Sisters at Cuckmere Haven.

Seven Sisters and cliff top path.

SUGGESTED WALK

WALK 9. Cuckmere Haven and the Seven Sisters (8.75 miles 14.1 km)

Parking. Park at the Exceat car park which is opposite the Visitor Centre (BN25 4AD). This is a long, strenuous walk with several steep climbs and three stiles. Be warned that near the start of Section 2 there is a gate that you need to go through that is safe but close to the cliff edge and the perspective of height and steep drop could affect people who suffer with acrophobia (irrational fear of heights). You can do this walk as a point-to-point and have a second car parked at Birling Gap (BN20 0AB) or between early May and early October you can return to Exceat from Birling Gap using the Eastbourne Sightseeing bus. This will make the walk 4.25 miles (6.8km) and you will see everything except the Exceat memorial stone. Refreshments are usually available from a van in Exceat car park.

1. From the entrance to the car park go through a wooden gate to the left of the information board and in a few yards, you reach a 4-way footpath sign. Follow the grassy path that curves around to the right, signed as 'Beach Trail', with hills on your left. The grassy path soon meets with a concrete access road and you continue with the meandering River Cuckmere on your right. Just continue ahead aiming for the beach with the Coastguard Cottages ahead on the other side of the river that you passed on walk 6. At a junction continue ahead through a gate and along a wide track. Go through another gate and ahead to reach the beach with the Coastguard Cottages on the other side; this is the only undeveloped river mouth on the Sussex coast. (You were standing to the right of the cottages on walk 6 with the Seven Sisters in view, they are now behind you; notice how close the cliff erosion is to the cottages.)

2. Go left along the beach and when you reach Cliff End go left through a gate and pass two 'pill-boxes' on your right. (This area was studied by the Luftwaffe during WWII as a possible landing site for the invasion of the UK.) About 120 yards past the 'pill-boxes' go right through a gate and immediately turn right and climb steeply up a wide grassy path. Climb to the top, keeping well away from the edge especially if you have children with

Coastguard Cottages by eroding cliff.

Common lizard.

Sheep enjoying the view.

you, going through a gate on the way which is close to the edge highlighting the steep drop. From the top appreciate the views back to Cuckmere Haven, Coastguard Cottages and towards Newhaven harbour; also keep a look out for lizards basking in this area. Cross a stile in a wire fence and continue to a 3-way footpath sign. Take the path that directs you right towards the cliff edge and then just continue along the cliff edge path with Belle Tout Lighthouse in view ahead on the other side of Birling Gap which you will pass on walk 10.

View from the top.

The path obviously goes up and down with some of the climbs being very steep and you keep to the path nearest the cliff edge for the best views; a lot of the paths are loose chalk so just pace yourself, there is no rush. (If you want to monitor which peak you are on the order is: Haven Brow, Short Brow, Rough Brow, Brass Point, Flagstaff Brow, Flat Hill, Baily's Hill & Went Hill). At Brass Point there is a National Trust information board telling you that you are now at the mid-way point.

Sarsen stone monument and plaque.

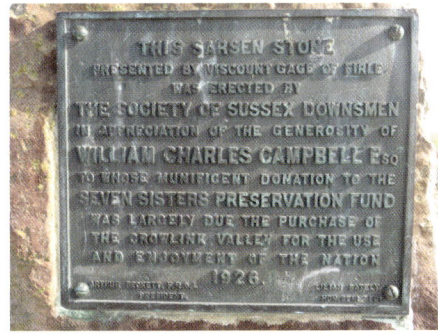

Soon you reach a Sarsen stone monument which commemorates William Charles Campbell who brought and donated this section of coastline to the nation; there is a plaque on it which you can read. Continue and soon you reach the obelisk Robertson War Memorial at Michel Dene.

Go through a gate at Went Hill with Birling Gap in view ahead. Go ahead along a wide path to reach a 3-way footpath sign. (If you are finishing at Birling Gap, go right and continue ahead to reach the car park at Birling Gap.)

3. Go left at the footpath sign saying East Dean 1 mile. Go through a gate and ahead over Went Hill with views back of where you have just walked. Go through a gate and continue ahead up a wide grassy path going to the left of a barn. Once past the barn remain in the same field and continue with a row of trees on your right. Pass a marker post and continue ahead with the trees on your right and in the far corner you reach a stone wall. Go left and go through a swing gate then continue ahead up a right field edge with a wire fence on your right. Just follow the wire fence ahead then around to the right to reach Crowlink car park. Follow the access road to reach the A259 with Friston church on the right and a pond on the left. Opposite are two roads, cross the main road and go up the road on the left (to the left of the green between the roads).

Robertson War Memorial.

4. Just 10 yards along this road go left into Friston Forest and in 5 yards go through a metal gate. Go ahead along the wide path with the A259 running parallel on your left about 30 yards away. Just follow the undulating/winding path, ignoring any side paths, just keeping the A259 on your left and being careful of the steep drop on your right. (There are actually two paths running close to the road, one is only about 5 yards

Friston Forest.

Cuckmere River.   Exceat memorial stone.

from it. Both will do but the one about 30 yards away is much quieter). Just keep going until the path reaches an access track. Continue ahead and soon, if you were using the path that was 30 yards from the road, you will join the path nearer the road and you keep going.

Now look carefully. When you reach a marker post on the left of the path pointing to the right, continue for another 100 yards to another junction. (Here you have the option to continue ahead, go to the right or take a minor path to the left to reach the A259 – don't worry if you miss it just keep going ahead to reach the Visitors Centre, you can't get lost.) Go left to the road and cross the stile opposite. Go ahead across a minor grassy path and in 20 yards you reach a grassy track. I have brought you this way for two reasons. Firstly, you can appreciate the River Cuckmere from an elevated height and secondly you can do an optional detour to visit the stone memorial for the long-lost village of Exceat.

If you want to finish the walk, go right and follow it round to the car park in view to the left of the Visitors Centre. To visit the stone memorial, go left along the path for a few hundred yards. Just before the path starts to descend to a stile in a fence the stone is about 10 yards on the right partially obscured by vegetation.

As you stand here looking down to the River Cuckmere try to imagine that Exceat was a bustling fishing village in Saxon times. It was also thought to be one of the most important naval bases for King Alfred. However, in the fourteenth century the Black Death arrived in 1347 and the village was all but wiped out as the disease arrived here by boat. The village also fell victim to attacks from French raiders and the few survivors had abandoned the village by the mid 1400s. All that remains is this stone marker that is on the site of Exceat church. It is surprising that the majority of people who visit this area regularly are completely unaware of the existence of this stone. It is off the normal paths and obscured by vegetation. It would be nice if it were signposted and perhaps an information board located close to it detailing Exceat's history or maybe we should start a campaign to get the memory of ancient Exceat back on the map?

Once you have visited the stone return the same way and follow the path back around to the car park.

CHAPTER 7
EAST DEAN, BIRLING GAP & BEACHY HEAD

EAST DEAN

East Dean lies in a steep valley on the South Downs close to Birling Gap and Beachy Head. The village was settled in early Saxon times initially by Aelle and his sons and then through the Kings of Wessex to Alfred the Great who had a manor here. The manor of Birling was very likely to have been in existence since Saxon times as a fishing and farming community with the village protected by the South Downs.

East Dean and Friston is a parish in the Wealden District of East Sussex. The two villages lie in a dry valley on the South Downs close to Birling Gap and Beachy Head. East Dean lies in the valley bottom and Friston is at the top of the hill to the west; both villages contain a large number of buildings of historic interest.

The church in East Dean is dedicated to St Simon and St Jude, it has a Saxon tower and an unusual Tapsel gate. (A Tapsel gate is a type of wooden gate that is unique to Sussex. It has a central pivot upon which it can rotate through 90 degrees in either direction before coming to a stop at two fixed points. It was named after a Sussex family of bell-founders, one of whom invented it in the late eighteenth century. Only six remain in the county and all are found within 10 miles of Lewes. They are easier for pallbearers to negotiate than a normal side-hinged gate: they can pass on each side and the coffin can be rested on the central pivot if necessary).

East Dean is where the world's most famous detective decided to retire to. Sherlock Holmes, the fictional detective, ended his career here to live by the sea. In the original stories he was said to have retired to a small farm on the South Downs where he spent his final years as a beekeeper. Although the precise location was never written down in the books a series of clues point to the tiny village of East Dean.

St Simon and St Jude church with Tapsel gate.

EAST DEAN, BIRLING GAP & BEACHY HEAD

 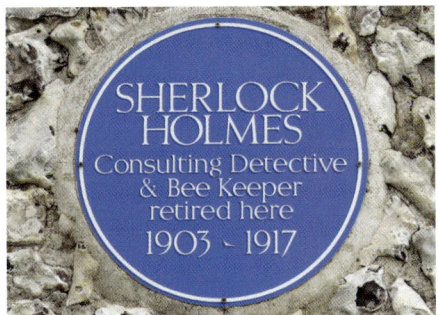

Sherlock Holmes's retirement cottage, East Dean.

East Dean sits just beyond Beachy Head and in one of his short stories, His Last Bow, author Sir Arthur Conan Doyle revealed that Holmes retired to a small farm 5 miles outside of Eastbourne; East Dean is just under 5 miles from Eastbourne's town centre. Conan Doyle was also believed to have visited East Dean having lived in nearby Crowborough in later life.

There is a blue plaque on the cottage in East Dean which is believed to be the actual place that Conan Doyle had in mind for Holmes' golden years and after more than 100 years on from the publication of His Last Bow, fans still hold sightseeing walks to get a glimpse of the cottage. Very close to the cottage on the other side of the green is the lovely Tiger Inn pub. The pub has been serving fine ales, wines and foods to local residents, farmers, soldiers and smugglers since the sixteenth century. Holmes's cottage and the Tiger Inn are visited on walk 10.

BIRLING GAP

Birling Gap is a coastal hamlet situated on the Seven Sisters near to Beachy Head. Coastal erosion has already claimed some of the row of coastguard cottages that were built on the cliff top in 1878; those that remain are currently still inhabited, but for how long? In time the houses are likely to be demolished due to the severe coastal erosion in this area as the Government has decided that the commercial value of the houses does not justify the construction of sea defences. There is a café, shop and visitor centre run by the National Trust and a metal staircase that leads down to the enclosed pebble beach with the Seven Sisters chalk cliffs to the west – passed on walk 9.

Cliff erosion at Birling Gap (08.03.18).

The beach was awarded the Blue Flag rural beach award in 2005 and is advertised by Naturist UK; a large number of rock pools can be found here. Noted artist Jean Cooke (1927-2008 an English painter of still life, landscapes, portraits and figures) lived in two cottages at Birling Gap; she painted seascapes there and died in 2008 while looking at the sea.

The main rock type at Birling Gap is Coombe Rock, which is a mixture of clay silt, flint and chalk. The coastline is part of the Site of Special Scientific Interest Seaford to Beachy Head and is of biological and geological interest.

Belle Tout Lighthouse.

The Belle Tout Lighthouse (occasionally spelt Belle Toute) is a decommissioned lighthouse and landmark located between Birling Gap and Beachy Head and is a prominent landmark from miles around. It has been called 'Britain's most famous inhabited lighthouse' because of its striking location on the cliff top and its use in film and television. In 1999 the Grade II listed building was relocated in one piece to prevent it succumbing to coastal erosion which is quite severe in this area.

The cliffs near Beachy Head saw many shipwrecks in the seventeenth and early eighteenth centuries and a petition to erect a lighthouse began around 1691. The calls were ignored for more than 100 years until *The Thames* an East Indiaman, crashed into the rocks at Beachy Head. The petition gained momentum with the support of a Captain of the Royal Navy and Trinity House (the official authority for lighthouses in England, Wales, the Channel Islands and Gibraltar) agreed to attend to the matter. Having witnessed the incident for himself, John 'Mad Jack' Fuller, MP for Sussex, used his influence and some of his own money to fund the lighthouse construction. The original Belle Tout Lighthouse was a temporary wooden structure that began service on 1 October 1828; it displayed a revolving light, which exhibited its greatest brilliancy once in two minutes.

The construction of the permanent granite lighthouse began in 1829 to a design by Thomas Stevenson and it became operational on 11 October 1834. The light was provided by a three-sided rotating array of lamps with ten lamps on each side, each lamp mounted within a parabolic reflector. Its use of 30 oil lamps meant the lighthouse would require two gallons of oil every hour. In 1887 the light was altered and it was equipped with the latest Douglass (Sir James Douglass 1826-1898 was an English civil engineer, a prolific lighthouse builder and designer, who was most famous for the design and construction of the fourth Eddystone Lighthouse, for which he was knighted) two-wick oil burners: six lamps and reflectors on each side of a clockwork-driven revolving triangular frame; 18 lamps in total. The speed of rotation was significantly increased to give a four second flash every fifteen seconds.

The lighthouse was not as successful as was hoped as the cliff-top location caused problems when sea mists obscured the light, significantly reducing the distance the light could reach. Ships that sailed too closely to the rocks would not be able to see the light because it was blocked by the cliff edge.

The Belle Tout was in service until 2 October 1902 when a new lighthouse was built at the bottom of the cliffs, known as the Beachy Head Lighthouse and Trinity House sold Belle Tout in 1903 after which time it changed hands several times.

During WWII the building was left empty; it was badly damaged by Canadian artillery fire, although the lighthouse was not the target: the guns were firing at wooden silhouettes of tanks which ran up the hill along rails to the east of the building.

The local council took ownership in 1948 and a decision was made to restore the lighthouse because of its historical significance. Building work was carried out under lease in 1956 and the lighthouse was brought up to date with modern amenities. In 1986 the BBC purchased the lease to Belle Tout for the filming of the mini-series *The Life and Loves of a She-Devil* and a year later it featured in the James Bond film *The Living Daylights*. From 1996 it was used as a family home and in 2007 the building was put up for sale again; it now includes six bedrooms and large walled gardens.

By 1999 the erosion of the cliffs was threatening the structure and on 17 March 1999 in a remarkable feat of engineering the Belle Tout was moved 17 metres (56ft) away from the cliff face. The 850-ton lighthouse was moved using a pioneering system of hydraulic jacks which pushed the building along four steel-topped concrete beams that were constantly lubricated with grease; the site should now be safe for many years to come.

In January 2010 the lighthouse was featured on Channel 5 in a programme named *Build a New Life in the Country*. This showed how it had been purchased in 2008 and converted into a luxury bed and breakfast. It had been bought for £500,000 and a further £700,000 was spent restoring it. The original access road was too close to the cliff edge so a payment of an easement fee to build a new road was negotiated with the local council.

Beachy Head Lighthouse is located in the English Channel below the cliffs of Beachy Head. It has a total height of 43m (141ft) and became operational in 1902. It was the last traditional-style 'rock-tower' (offshore lighthouse) to be built by Trinity House.

In 1902 under the direction of Sir Thomas Matthews, the Trinity House Engineer-in-Chief, the present lighthouse was brought into service, sited about 165 metres seawards from the base of the cliffs. It took two years to complete and involved building a cofferdam (a watertight enclosure

Beachy Head Lighthouse.

pumped dry to permit construction work below the waterline) and a temporary cable car from the top of the cliffs to carry workers and materials down to the site was installed; 3660 tons of Cornish granite were used in the construction of the tower.

The Beachy Head Lighthouse was built to replace Belle Tout and was equipped with a first-order catadioptric optic (one where refraction and reflection are combined in an optical system, usually via lenses [dioptrics] and curved mirrors [catoptrics]) made up of three double panels, giving two white flashes every twenty seconds; the light source was a Matthews-designed paraffin vapour burner. The new lighthouse was also provided with an explosive fog signal which was sounded every five minutes in foggy weather; it involved the keepers attaching a small explosive charge together with a detonator to each arm of a jib located on the gallery of the lighthouse; when winched into place, connection was made with a dynamo-electric firing machine inside the lantern, from where the charge was remotely fired.

For more than eighty years the red and white striped tower was manned by three lighthouse keepers; their primary job being to maintain the revolving light, which was visible for 26 nautical miles (30 mi, 48 km) out to sea. For most of the twentieth century cooking was done on a solid-fuel range and the accommodation was lit by paraffin lamps; electricity was introduced in 1975 whereupon an electric lamp was used in the optic. The explosive fog signal remained until 1976 when it was replaced by an 'ELG 500' electric emitter; at that time Beachy Head was one of the last lighthouses still using explosive signals. The lighthouse was fully automated in 1983 and in June 1983 the keepers withdrawn.

In 2011 Trinity House announced that it could no longer afford to repaint the red and white stripes and that it would have to be left to return to its natural granite grey. It said that because boats now have high tech navigational systems that the day marker stripes are no longer essential. However, a sponsored campaign to keep the stripes was launched in October 2011. The required £27,000 was raised and the tower repainting was completed in October using a team including two abseilers. Five coats of paint were applied to the copper lantern at the top and three on each hoop of the tower. The lighthouse's aids to navigation were converted to solar power operation in 2011 and further upgrades to the navigation light, control system and the solar power system were carried out in 2018.

BEACHY HEAD

Beachy Head is a chalk headland situated close to Eastbourne and immediately east of the Seven Sisters. The cliff is the highest chalk sea cliff in Britain and it rises to 162 metres (531 ft) above sea level. The peak allows views of the south east coast towards Dungeness in the east and the Isle of Wight in the west. On a completely negative note, its height has also made it one of the most common suicide spots in the world; with around 20 suicides per year.

The chalk was formed in the Late Cretaceous epoch between 66 and 100 million years ago, when the area was under the sea; during the Cenozoic Era the chalk was uplifted. When the last Ice Age ended the sea levels rose and the English Channel formed, cutting into the chalk to form the dramatic cliffs along the Sussex coast. Wave action contributes towards the erosion of the cliffs around Beachy Head, which experience frequent small rock falls. As chalk forms in layers separated by contiguous bands of flints, the physical structure affects how the cliffs erode. Wave action undermines the lower cliffs, causing frequent slab failures – slabs from layers of chalk break off, causing the upper parts of the cliffs to eventually collapse. A mass movement happened in 2001 when after a winter of heavy rain, the water had begun to seep into the cracks which had frozen and caused the cracks to widen; this then made the cliff edge erode and collapse into the sea, destroying a well-known chalk stack called the Devil's Chimney.

The name Beachy Head appears as 'Beauchef' in 1274, becoming 'Beaucheif' by 1317 and it has nothing to do with the word beach; instead, it is a corruption of the original French words meaning 'beautiful headland' (beau chef). It was constantly referred to as Beachy Head by 1724.

On the 5 August 1895 the German social scientist and philosopher Friedrich Engels, one of the fathers of communism, died of laryngeal cancer in London. Following cremation has ashes were scattered off Beachy Head as he had requested.

In the 1950s human remains were discovered which were later subjected to forensic reconstruction, carbon dating and radioisotope analysis and they were found to be those of a Roman woman of Sub-Saharan African origin who grew up in the Eastbourne area in about 200-250 CE (Common Era). She has become known as Beachy Head Lady.

During WWII the Royal Air Force established a forward relay station at Beachy Head to improve radio communications with aircraft. In 1942, signals were picked up which were identified as TV transmissions from the Eiffel Tower. The Germans had reactivated the pre-war TV transmitter and instated a Franco-German service for military hospitals and VIPs in the Paris region. The RAF monitored these programmes, hoping, in vain, to gather intelligence from newsreels.

Standing proud on Beachy Head is a 7-ton memorial that pays tribute to those brave airmen who flew during WWII under Bomber Command. The memorial is in a very significant place on Beachy Head as it was the flightpath for the Lancaster Bombers and for many airmen it was their last sight of England.

Bomber Command Memorial.

Now you can do the walk that begins by the Tiger Inn and Sherlock Holmes's retirement cottage before setting out through Birling Gap to Beachy Head passing both lighthouses. I will see you at Eastbourne.

SUGGESTED WALK

WALK 10. East Dean, Sherlock Holmes' Cottage, Birling Gap and Beachy Head. (8.25 miles 13.3 km)

Parking. There is free parking at the car park in Village Green Lane off Gilberts Drive (Post code BN20 0DJ). This is the toughest walk in the book but in my opinion, it is one of the best. There are a number of long steep climbs (the longest and steepest being near the end) and you can be exposed to strong winds when walking beside the cliffs but there are no stiles. Refreshments are available from the Tiger Inn (start/finish) at East Dean, The Beachy Head pub and there is a café and toilets at Birling Gap.

To give you some idea about the severity of coastal erosion in this area – I did this walk on 10 August 2021, 8 days earlier a large cliff collapse just east of Belle Tout took out part of the official footpath.

PLEASE NOTE there are three ways that you can do this walk. 1 - In total as a tough 8.25 mile circular. 2 - Using two cars, one at East Dean and the other at a Beachy Head car park near the Beachy Head pub. 3 - Car at East Dean and between beginning of May and beginning of Oct (check their website) you can return from Beachy Head, having seen all the points off interest, on the Eastbourne Sightseeing bus which stops back at the Tiger Inn at East Dean. These will reduce the walk to 4.5 miles (7.2 km).

1. From the car park, go over to the green signpost that shows all the local attractions and go right to the Tiger Inn which is only 20 yards up on the right. From the pub go across the green, passing a war memorial and a cottage on the right which is supposed to be the place where Sherlock Holmes retired; there is a blue plaque on the wall.

Tiger Inn and War Memorial, East Dean.

On the far side go left along Upper Street then continue along Went Way with houses on the right. Go to the end of Went Way and go through a wide metal gate by a bridleway sign. Follow the grassy path to a wooden bridle gate; go through the gate and ahead with a wire fence on your left. Just follow the path, climbing quite steeply to reach a marker post near the top by open grassland. Go left around the field edge aiming for a brick building. Go to the right of the building, go through a metal gate and ahead down a wide grassy path with Birling Gap and Belle Tout on your left. At the bottom of the path go through a gate and continue ahead. Go through another gate and follow the path down and around

Birling Gap cliff erosion (10.08.21).

The Seven Sisters from Birling Gap.

to the left to reach Birling Gap. At Birling Gap take the opportunity to go to the cliff edge where there is access to the beach. The cliffs here are badly eroding and more houses are in danger of falling into the sea. From this area you get a lovely view back towards the Seven Siters that you walked in the last chapter.

2. From the car park go ahead by a telephone box and 3-way footpath sign for the South Downs Way. Go up steps and continue ahead aiming for Belle Tout Lighthouse. (SAFETY- if you have children with you keep them well away from the eroding cliff edge and be careful of your footing all the way to the Beachy Head pub. There are areas of erosion and many animal burrows along the route.) Pass to the left of Belle Tout Lighthouse and continue ahead using the cliff edge path now heading for Beachy Head Lighthouse which is in view at the bottom of the cliff; you get lovely views from the cliff top but don't get too close to the edge. Just follow the obvious path passing Beachy Head Lighthouse and continuing to Beachy Head pub. Take regular looks behind you to admire your efforts so far.

As you reach the pub look out for the various memorials including the Watch Tower and there is a trig point here as well for those of you that like to photograph/record them. Just before the pub you will see a concrete path that goes over to a vantage point to the right from where you will get lovely views back towards Birling Gap, a really good view of Eastbourne at the end of the South Downs Way and at the vantage point is the Bomber Command memorial. Now you can head over to the Beachy Head pub for a well-deserved drink or five. (From here you can return using the Eastbourne Sightseeing open-top bus which stops here between early May and early October to the Tiger Inn.)

Beachy Head Lighthouse.

Watch Tower memorial.

3. Leave the pub and turn right (heading back) along the road using the left-hand pavement/verge at first and then the grassy path that runs a few yards to the left of the road. Soon you will reach a parking area where the road bends sharply to the right; continue ahead (now away from the road) aiming to the right of a clump of trees with Belle Tout in view ahead. Keep to the right of the trees and just past them the path begins to descend.

Memorial at Beachy Head.

Go right and descend down a left field edge aiming for the road at the bottom (you can see your onward path directly ahead rising on the opposite side of the road).

Cross the road and go ahead by a wide metal gate and a footpath sign signed East Dean Down 2 miles. Follow the right field edge which soon curves to the right to reach a gate and stile in the far corner. Go through the gate and ahead up a right field edge now signed as East Dean 2 miles. At the top go through two gates (1 metal, 1 wood) and continue ahead up a right field edge. On the far side go left for 15 yards then right through a strip of trees and continue to a gate in the field corner. Go through the gate and go up and ahead across the next field on a faint path to a gate in view. Go through the gate and diagonally left to a 3-way footpath sign that is in view a short distance away.

As indicated go down the track, signed Warren Hill, and follow it as it curves around to the left passing a dew pond and then a solitary Water Treatment Works building. About 150 yards past the Water Treatment Works go right through a bridle gate which is a few yards past the footpath sign.

Go up a right field edge, with a barbed-wire fence on your right, to the left of New Barn – this is a very steep climb, particularly after what you have already accomplished; take your time and relish the fact that this is your final climb of any significance. Go through a gate at the top and ahead along a left field edge for a short distance, then continue with a fence on your right aiming for Friston ahead.

New Barn.

On the far side go through a gate by a 4-way footpath sign and go ahead with a fence on your left to reach the A259. Turn left along the road using the right-hand verge then pavement. In about 150 yards, cross back over the A259 and go left down Gilberts Drive. In 70 yards go right along Village Green Lane to the car park and Tiger Inn – Well Done.

CHAPTER 8
EASTBOURNE

Eastbourne is a town and popular seaside resort located immediately to the east of Beachy Head the highest chalk sea cliff in Great Britain and which is part of the larger Eastbourne Downland Estate.

The seafront consists mainly of Victorian hotels, a pier, a state-of-the-art theatre, a contemporary art gallery and a Napoleonic era fort and military museum. Eastbourne was developed at the direction of the Duke of Devonshire from 1859 from four separate hamlets and today it is a thriving town with a modernised town centre with a large shopping centre called 'The Beacon' and an extensive high street. The town grew as a fashionable tourist resort largely due to William Cavendish who later became the Duke of Devonshire. He appointed architect Henry Currey to design a street plan for the town after sending him to Europe to draw inspiration. The resulting mix of architecture is mainly Victorian which is still a key feature of Eastbourne. As a seaside resort, Eastbourne derives a large and increasing income from tourism with revenue from popular seaside attractions.

Five Star Grand Hotel.

Eastbourne seafront architecture.

Flint mines and Stone Age artefacts have been discovered in the countryside of the Eastbourne Downs, a Bronze Age site of national importance was discovered in Hydneye Lake at Shinewater Park in 1995 and Celtic people are believed to have settled on the Eastbourne Downland in 500BC.

There are Roman remains buried beneath the town, which include a Roman bath and a section of pavement between Eastbourne Pier and the Redoubt Fortress. There is also a Roman villa near the entrance to the pier and the present Queens Hotel.

An Anglo-Saxon charter c963 AD describes a landing stage and stream at Burne (meaning brook or stream). The original name came from the 'Burne' or stream which ran through todays Old Town area of Eastbourne; today all that can be seen of the Burne or Bourne is the small pond in Motcombe Gardens. Motcombe Gardens are overlooked by St Mary's church which is a Norman church that allegedly lies on the site of a Saxon 'moot', or meeting place.

In 2014 a local metal-detectorist found a unique coin minted during the reign of Æthelberht II of East Anglia (died 794), in a field near the town. The silver coin gives a clue to Æthelberht's beheading by Offa of Mercia, as it had been struck as a sign of independence. Coin expert Christopher Webb said 'This new discovery is an important and unexpected addition to the numismatic history of eighth century England'. The 1200-year-old coin went up for auction on 11 June 2014 with a pre-sale estimate of £15,000 - £20,000. After fierce bidding in the sale room and on-line the price shot up to £65,000 won by an internet bidder. After buyer's commission was added the winning bidder paid £78,000.

Following the Norman conquest, the Hundred of what is now Eastbourne, was held by Robert, Count of Mortain, William the Conqueror's half-brother. The Domesday Book lists 28 ploughlands, a church, a watermill, fisheries and salt pans. The book referred to the area as 'Bourne'; 'East' was added to 'Bourne' in the thirteenth century, renaming the town.

A charter for a weekly market was granted to Bartholomew de Badlesmere in 1315-16 which increased his status as Lord of the Manor and improved local industry. During the Middle Ages the town was visited by King Henry I and in 1324 by Edward II. Eastbourne's medieval past can be seen in the twelfth century church of St Mary and the manor house called Bourne Place. In the mid-sixteenth century Bourne Place was home to the Burton family who acquired much of the land on which the present town stands. The manor house is currently owned by the Duke of Devonshire and was extensively remodelled in the early Georgian era when it was renamed Compton Place. It is one of two Grade I listed building in the town.

In 1752 a dissertation by Doctor Richard Russell praised the medicinal benefits of the seaside. His views were of great benefit to the south coast and in time Eastbourne became known as 'the Empress of Watering Places'. Eastbourne's earliest claim as a seaside resort came about following a summer holiday visit by four of King George III's children in 1780; Princes Edward, Octavius and Princesses Elizabeth and Sophia all visited.

In 1793, following a survey of coastal defences in the southeast, approval was given for the positioning of infantry and artillery to defend the bay between Beachy Head and Hastings from attack by the French. Martello Towers were constructed

View east towards Sovereign Harbour.

along the western shore of Pevensey Bay, continuing as far as Tower 73, the Wish Tower, at Eastbourne. Between 1805-07 construction took place of a fortress known as Eastbourne Redoubt which was built as a barracks and storage depot armed with ten cannons.

By the mid-nineteenth century most of the area was in the hands of two landowners: John Davies Gilbert (the Davies-Gilbert family still own much of the land in Eastbourne and East Dean) and William Cavendish, Earl of Burlington. The Gilbert family's holdings date to the late seventeenth and early eighteenth centuries when barrister Nicholas Gilbert married an Eversfield and Gildredge heiress; the Gildredges owned much of Eastbourne by 1554. The Gilberts eventually made the Gildredge Manor House their own and today the Gildredge name lives on in the eponymous park.

View west towards Wish Tower.

On 14 May 1849 the London, Brighton and South Coast Railway arrived and the town's growth accelerated. Cavendish who was now the 7th Duke of Devonshire, recruited Henry Currey in 1859 to lay out a plan for what was an entire new town – a resort built 'for gentlemen by gentlemen'. The town grew rapidly and a purpose-built town hall was opened in 1886. This growth and elegant development continued for several decades and there was a royal visit by George V and Queen Mary in 1935.

During WWI, Summerdown Camp, a convalescent facility was opened in 1915 near the South Downs to treat soldiers who were injured during trench warfare or were seriously ill. It was the largest of this type in the UK during this war and it treated 150,000 of which 80% were able to return to fight. The facility was dismantled in 1920.

WWII saw a change in fortunes. Initially children were evacuated to Eastbourne as it was assumed they would be safe from German bombs, but soon they had to be evacuated again because after the fall of France in June 1940 it was anticipated that the town would lie in an invasion zone. Part of Operation Sea Lion, the German invasion plan, envisaged landings at Eastbourne and many people sought safety away from the coast having shut up their houses. The Royal Navy set up an underwater weapons school and the Royal Air Force operated radar stations at Beachy Head and on the marshes near Pevensey. Thousands of Canadian soldiers were billeted in and around Eastbourne from July 1941 to the run-up to D-Day. Eastbourne suffered badly with many Victorian and Edwardian buildings damaged or destroyed by air raids and by the end of the conflict it was designated by the Home Office to have been 'the most raided town in the South East region'. It was especially bad between May 1942 and June 1943 with hit-and-run raids from fighter-bombers based in northern France. Ultimately 187 civilian lives were lost in the borough through enemy action.

After the war, development continued and in the 1990s growth and controversy accelerated rapidly as a new plan was launched to develop the area known as the Crumbles, a shingle bank on the coast to the east of the town centre. This area is now known as Sovereign Harbour and contains a marina, shops, several thousand houses and luxury flats but it was formerly the home to many rare plants, hence the controversy. Just the other side of Sovereign Harbour is Martell. Tower No. 64 which is on the beach and reached on walk 11.

In 2009, the Towner Gallery was opened in College Road. It hosts one of the most significant public art collections in the South of England and attracts over 100,000 visitors a year. It was described by ITV news as 'the region's biggest art gallery' in 2017. It was established with a bequest in 1920, from John Chisholm Towner who had served as a local alderman. Initially it was homed in Manor Gardens, adjacent to Gildredge Park in the Old Town. Opening in 1923, it closed when the building was sold in 2005. In 2009 it re-opened in a purpose-built facility adjacent to the Congress Theatre near the seafront.

A major tourist event held annually is the Eastbourne Airbourne also known as the Eastbourne International Airshow. It is a four-day international air show run every August in Eastbourne. The event features Battle of Britain memorial flights and aircraft from the RAF and USAF, among others and enjoys a long relationship with the Red Arrows display team. The event started in 1993 and is free. Although, the Eastbourne seafront is the usual place to sit and watch the display. On 15 August 2003 I was doing a walk that took me to Beachy Head totally unaware that it was the air show weekend. You can imagine my surprise as wing-walkers on biplanes, bombers and the Red Arrows, to name but a few

Sovereign Harbour.

Towner Gallery (Sep 2021).

Red Arrow at Eastbourne Airshow 2003.

were flying just overhead. It was a great bonus and the area around the Beachy Head pub was packed.

Eastbourne Bandstand is the busiest bandstand in the UK that offers a variety of live musical entertainment with over 140 events each year ranging from Tribute Shows to 1812 Fireworks concerts to kids entertainment. The current bandstand with its unique semi-circular design and blue domed roof was built in 1935 and there in no

Eastbourne Bandstand.

other like it in the UK. It has a main arena, middle and upper balconies and 1400 seats. The building of the bandstand formed part of the main seafront improvements and cost £28,000 to build and was surmounted with a stainless-steel spire. The project engineer was Leslie Rosevere. The first concerts were on 28 July 1935 with a total of 10,400 attending all three concerts and paying 3d each. It was officially opened on 5 August 1935 by the Lord Lieutenant of the county, Lord Leconfield with an audience of 8000.

There is a commemorative (three-section) plaque opposite the bandstand in the main arena in memory of Eastbourne bandsman John Wesley Woodward, who was one of those playing on the *Titanic* when it sank on 15 April 1912. The bandstand has featured in numerous TV programmes and films such as *Foyle's War*, *Little Britain* and BBC *Antiques Roadshow*.

Eastbourne Pier was built between 1866 and 1872. In April 1865 the Eastbourne Pier Company was formed with a working capital of £15,000. Work began in April 1866 and four years later on 13 June 1870 Lord Edward Cavendish opened the pier although it wasn't completed until 1872. The pier is 984 feet (300m) long and built on stilts which rest in cups on the seabed which allows the whole structure to move during rough weather.

The pier's entrance was originally built on the lower promenade but due to rough storms in 1877 it was swept away so the rebuild was at a higher

Commemorative plaque to bandsman John Wesley Woodward.

level, creating a drop towards the end of the pier. In 1888 a 400-seater domed pavilion was built at a cost of £250 at the seaward end and two years later a 1000-seater theatre, bar, camera obscura and office suite replaced it. The same year two saloons were built midway along the pier.

During WWII decking was removed to host machine guns to provide a useful advantage point to repel enemy landings. In December 1942 an exploding mine caused considerable damage to the pier and nearby hotels; it had been tied to the stanchions by the local police who were under the mistaken impression that it was fitted with a safety device.

Eastbourne Pier.

In 1970 the 1000 seat theatre was destroyed by fire in an arson attack; it was replaced with an evening entertainment venue that has since become home to Atlantis Nightclub called The Waterfront Café/Bar. On 30 July 2014 the pier caught fire again destroying the large arcade and saloons in the middle. BBC News reported that 80 firefighters attended the blaze but one third of the pier was badly damaged. After this the buildings were dismantled and it was made into an 'open-deck' area. Mr Sheikh Abid Gulzar a local hotelier bought the pier in November 2015 and in the short time that he has owned it he has renovated the pier including re-painting, adding 20 new benches to the open deck area and provided entertainment for visitors.

Eastbourne Redoubt on Royal Parade was built to keep Napoleon's armies out of Britain in the early nineteenth century and for over 200 years it has stood ready to defend the Eastbourne coast. Forming part of a chain of fortifications built to deter Napoleon's forces it was garrisoned by troops until the early 1900s and again during WWII.

Construction of the Redoubt Fortress was handled by William Hobson with the work starting in 1804 until 1810, using five million bricks which were shipped on barges down the east coast from London. It is made up of 24 Casemates (a small room in the wall of a fortress, with openings from which guns or missiles can be fired) placed in a ring 220ft (67m) in diameter, surrounded by a moat 25ft wide by 24ft deep; due to the Redoubt standing on shingle the moat could never be filled. The only entrance was across a bridge which linked the gun platform with the inland face of the fortress. The sea-facing side is protected with a layer of shingle mixed with cement to help the building survive canon fire from enemy ships. The interior of the fortress is on two levels, the upper-level being the gun platform and the lower-level accommodation for up to 350 soldiers.

EASTBOURNE

Redoubt Fortress and museum.

Martello Tower No. 73 (Wish Tower).

The Redoubt is open between April and mid-November with access to the parade ground, gun platform and regimental museums and is passed on walk 11.

Eastbourne has two Martello Towers along its seafront and both are passed on walk 11. Tower No. 73 known as the Wish Tower is west of the pier in a park by Western Parade. Tower No. 66 is to the east of the pier on the beach by the breakwater/ entrance to Sovereign Harbour.

Martello Tower No. 66.

Sovereign Harbour is a development of the beach-land on the far eastern side of Eastbourne near Pevensey. Opened in 1993 and formerly known as The Crumbles, the marina now consists of five separate harbours (North Harbour, South Harbour, West Harbour, Outer Harbour and Inner Harbour), a retail park and several housing projects. It is Northern Europe's largest composite marina complex.

The tidal Outer Harbour is only used for entrance to the marina through twin sea locks which are operated 24 hours a day. It needs frequent dredging to keep the access channel from the sea to the locks open and deep enough for vessels. The local RNLI lifeboat has its own mooring there. All the other harbours (Inner, South, West and North) are artificial and were dredged one after the other, after 1991.

Behind the locks is the main marina called Inner Harbour; it is the central body of water and was the first harbour in use. It contains berths for visiting and resident berth holders and also provides access to the other three harbours via lifting bridges; the other three being used mainly by resident berth holders and local fishing vessels.

The North Harbour is the latest development and is larger than the initial Inner Harbour. The two remaining harbours West and South are much smaller and are used by local residents who own a house or apartment around these waters.

The marina is also home for the Eastbourne lifeboat. The Tamar class all weather lifeboat, named *Diamond Jubilee* 16-23 is normally anchored in the Outer Harbour but can occasionally be seen moored in one of the locks during bad weather conditions; in this case, locking procedures make sure that the lifeboat can still launch at very short notice. The harbour has also attracted several wildlife visitors including four grey seals.

Finally, for any of you who enjoy walking (which I guess most of you do as you have bought this book – thank you and I hope you are enjoying it), Eastbourne is the start/finish of the 100-mile (161 km) Eastbourne to Winchester walk, the South Downs Way (SDW). The starting point is in Foyle Way by Dukes Drive and there are two potential routes. One option is the coastal route from Eastbourne to Alfriston and is for walkers only at 11 miles (17.5 km) or the second option is the slightly shorter inland route which is a bridleway section and runs from Eastbourne to Alfriston via Jevington at 7.5 miles (12 km).

I have never walked the whole length of the SDW but I have walked many sections of it and have twice done the section between Eastbourne and Alfriston. Both times I used the coastal route; it may be longer but the 530 feet high cliffs of Beachy Head provide stunning views across Eastbourne and the English Channel.

Now you can do the Eastbourne walk(s) to visit the, pier, bandstand, 3 Martello Towers, Redoubt Fort and Sovereign Harbour. I will see you inland at Herstmonceux to visit the Observatory and Castle.

Eastbourne from start of SDW: just 100 miles to go – good luck, or a few yards to go if you are finishing – well done.

SUGGESTED WALK

WALK 11. Pier, 3 Martello Towers, & Sovereign Harbour
11 miles 17.7 km)

Parking. Park wherever you like or arrive by bus or train. Please note that this is a long coastal walk but it has been written so that you can do it in two parts. Part 1 is going west from the pier and is sections 1 and 2 (4.5 miles) and part 2 is going east from the pier sections 3 and 4 (6.5 miles). Eastbourne is a large town so visiting twice will give you more chance to explore and sample the restaurants and pubs, but you can do the whole walk in one go. There are only a couple of short steep climbs on section 1, the rest is level with no stiles. Like Brighton there are hundreds of places to get refreshments so don't try to do a pub crawl.

1. (Part 1 – West 4.5 miles 7.2 km) With your back to the pier go left along the seafront; you can use the lower or middle path, to reach the bandstand in sight. (When you reach the bandstand remember to look out for the memorial plaque for John Wesley Woodward who died on the *Titanic* 15th April 1912, he was a musician who played at the Winter Gardens and the Grand Hotel as a member of the Duke of Devonshire Band. The memorial is on the back wall of the lower level opposite the bandstand.)

Eastbourne Bandstand.

From the bandstand continue to reach Martello Tower No. 73 (Wish Tower) which is in view ahead on top of a hill. When you look around the tower notice the civilian war memorial which is a plaque on the large rock by the tower.

Civilian War Memorial.

From the tower continue heading west using the lower path beside the beach. Immediately you can see the white cliffs ahead near Beachy Head and you can identify the starting path of the South Downs Way that rises to the right of the cliffs. Keep walking until you reach an access road (Holywell Drive) signed to Beachy Head, there are also a row of beachfront buildings numbered 37-42. Climb quite steeply to the top of the access road to

The SDW starts to the right of the cliffs.

Starting point of SDW.

reach Dukes Drive. Go left to reach the start of the South Downs Way (SDW) which is in view (writing a walk book for East Sussex I couldn't not take you to the start/end of what is one of the most famous walking routes in the south of England).

2. From the start of the SDW return back along Dukes Drive heading back past the Martello Tower and bandstand to arrive back at the pier. Along the way you can admire the seafront architecture and en-route you pass the Grand Hotel which is a Five Star hotel that has been described as a 'Palace by the Sea'. Continue to arrive back at the pier. (If you are doing this walk in two parts this is the opportunity for you to go and explore Eastbourne town.)

3. (Part 2 – East 6.5 miles 10.5 km). To continue the walk (or start part 2) go east (with the sea on your right) from the pier heading for the Redoubt Fortress and Museum. Just before the fort the road (Royal Parade) curves inland and runs behind the fort and the entrance to the fort is along this road which you can visit now or near the end of the walk. Continue along Royal Parade passing a bowling green and other attractions as you go and always knowing that the sea is just out of view on your right. Keep going and soon you reach Princes Park on your left which is a Green Flag award winning park that features a range of gardens, boating lake and wildlife and it is well worth a visit.

Grand Hotel.

Continue along the road to reach a roundabout and go right, past the Sovereign Centre, and continue along Prince William Parade. Soon you reach Sovereign Park

Fort Redoubt.

Princes Park.

Nature Reserve on your right. The Park aims to preserve some of the shingle beach habitat that was once common along the south coast until the increase in urban development and other pressures. The best time to visit is May and June as the land becomes very parched in midsummer; the flora and fauna associated with the rare shingle habitat is a must see and you will see it from both sides as you pass the other side on your return journey.

At the end you reach a roundabout with the next Martello Tower No. 66 behind it. Go right and in a few yards go left along the beach to reach the tower. Immediately behind the tower you reach the entrance to Sovereign Harbour by the two breakwaters and this area is very popular with fishermen casting their lines from the rocks. Go left here and walk into the harbour beside the harbourside flats on a there-and-back route to explore the harbour and Martello Tower No. 64 which is just past the harbour on the beach.

4. After exploring the actual harbour continue east (one mile return in total) going to the left of the Sovereign Harbour Marine Reception and walk beside the harbour-front residences. Just follow the path around to re-join the beach and continue to reach Martello Tower No. 64. Return the same way back through the marina to arrive back at Martello Tower No. 66. Now follow the seafront path all the way back to the pier which is in view way in the distance. The path is interrupted en-route by one small section that is along a short length of road but it quickly re-joins the seafront path. On the way you re-pass the other side of Sovereign Park Nature Reserve and the Redoubt Fort if you didn't visit it on your outward journey.

Martello Tower No. 66 beside the sea.

Martello Tower No. 64 just past the harbour.

CHAPTER 9
HERSTMONCEUX

Herstmonceux is a village north of Eastbourne. Historically the village was known as Gardner Street and the village name was adopted from the name of the nearby castle where, apparently, in the twelfth century a Saxon lady by the name of Idonea de Herst married a Norman nobleman called Ingelram de Monceux. The village is part of the larger Herstmonceux civil parish which includes Cowbeech, and the hamlets of Foul Mile, Trolliloes, Cowbeech Hill, Stunts Green, Ginger's Green, Flowers Green and part of Windmill Hill. The Herstmonceux Medieval Festival is held annually at the castle on the August Bank Holiday.

In 1677 Thomas Lennard, 1st Earl of Sussex was paid £3 when he went to a cricket match played at 'ye Dicker', a common near Herstmonceux, this is one of the earliest references to the sport.

The village is also famous for its Royal Sussex Trugs (baskets made from split willow boards set in an ash or chestnut frame). The Royal association is because the inventor of the trug, Thomas Smith, sold some personally to Queen Victoria at the Great Exhibition in Hyde Park in London 1851. A number of local people and businesses (including Thomas Smith's Trug Shop which moved to New Road, Magham Down, BN27 1PN) still continue this tradition.

Thomas Smith's Trug shop and traditional workshop.

There are two Sites of Special Scientific Interest within the parish. Herstmonceux Park is of importance because of its wetland habitat and fen vegetation and it is the only known location of milk parsley in the south-east. The other site is Pevensey Levels which lies partially within the parish but will be described in the next chapter at Pevensey; the site is of biological interest consisting of low-lying grazing meadows that contain a wide variety of wetland flora and fauna.

Herstmonceux is famous for its magnificent moated castle which is a Grade II listed building set in parkland

and Elizabethan gardens. It was originally built as a country home in the mid-fifteenth century and it embodies the history of medieval England and the romance of Renaissance Europe.

Herstmonceux was a significant place long before the castle was built. There is evidence of Roman remains and, as already mentioned, in the twelfth century a Saxon lady, Idonea de Herst married a Norman nobleman, Ingelram de Monceux giving the village its name. The name of the castle owners changed through marriage to Fiennes and the family increased in wealth and power; James Fiennes distinguished himself by fighting for King Henry V at the battle of Agincourt and later became sheriff of Surrey and Sussex.

By 1911 the castle had deteriorated into a ruin when it was bought by Lt Col Claude Lowther who used local craftsmen to carry out building work and by 1912 most of the south front was rebuilt. After the death of Col Lowther in 1929, Sir Paul Latham contributed greatly to the construction of the castle both internally and externally. In 1946 he sold it to the Admiralty who bought the estate for the Royal Greenwich Observatory and it became an important scientific institution for the next forty years.

Herstmonceux Castle one of the oldest significant brick buildings still standing in England. The castle was known for being one of the first buildings to use this material in England and it was built using bricks taken from the local clay by builders from Flanders. Dating from 1441 the construction began under the then-owner Sir Roger Fiennes and was continued after his death in 1449 by his son Lord Dacre. The parks and gardens of Herstmonceux Castle and Place are Grade II listed on the Register of Historic Parks and Gardens. Other listed structures on the estate include the Grade II listed walled garden to the north of the castle and the Grade II listed telescopes and workshops of the Herstmonceux Science Centre.

Herstmonceux Castle.

The first written evidence of the existence of the Herst settlement is in the Domesday Book which reports that one of William's closest supporters granted tenancy of the manor at Herst to a man named 'Wilbert'. By the end of the twelfth century, the family at the manor house at Herst had considerable status. Written accounts mention a lady called Idonea de Herst, who married a Norman nobleman named Ingelram de Monceux. Around this time the manor began to be called the 'Herst of the Monceux', a name that eventually became Herstmonceux.

A descendent of the Monceux family, Roger Fiennes was responsible for the construction of the castle as he had been appointed Treasurer of the Household of Henry VI and needed a house fitting a man of his position. Construction of the castle on the site of the old manor house began in 1441 and it was his position as Treasurer which enabled him to afford the £3800 cost of the original castle.

The castle changed ownership many times over the years and it gradually fell into ruin until it was dismantled in 1777 leaving the exterior walls standing and it remained a ruin until the early twentieth century.

In 1913 radical restoration work was undertaken by Colonel Claude Lowther to transform the ruin into a residence and based on a design by architect, Walter Godfrey, the work was completed by Paul Latham in 1933; the existing interiors largely date from that period and incorporate architectural antiques from England and France. The one major change in planning was the combination of the four internal courtyards into one large one. The restoration work, which was regarded as the apex of Godfrey's architectural achievement, was described by the critic Sir Nikolaus Pevsner as executed 'exemplarily'.

Herstmonceux Place is an eighteenth century country house that stands within a 148 hectares (370 acres) shared estate with Herstmonceux Castle; in the 1950s it was divided into apartments. Herstmonceux Place is a Grade I listed building and the gardens and parks of Herstmonceux Place and Castle are Grade II listed on the Register of Historic Parks and Gardens. Herstmonceux Place is passed on walk 12.

The Royal Observatory was founded by King Charles II at Greenwich in 1675. The observing conditions deteriorated following the urban growth of London and plans were made in the twentieth century to relocate the observatory to a rural location with clearer, darker skies. Herstmonceux Castle and estate were up for sale by their private owners and were sold in 1946 to the Admiralty, which at that time operated the Royal Observatory on behalf of the government. The relocation of the observatory took place over a decade and was completed by 1957; a number of new buildings were erected in the castle grounds. The institution at Herstmonceux Castle was known as the Royal Greenwich Observatory, where it remained until 1988 when the observatory relocated to Cambridge.

Several telescopes remain but the largest one, the 100-inch (254 cm) aperture Isaac Newton Telescope, was moved to La Palma in the Canary Islands in the

Herstmonceux Observatory.

1970s as it became clear that better astronomical weather conditions would benefit its use. The estate provides housing for the Equatorial Telescope Buildings, which have been converted for use as an interactive science centre for schoolchildren. The empty dome for the Newton Telescope remains on the site and is a landmark that is visible from afar.

The observatory needs to be visited to fully appreciate it and my thanks to the manager, Laura Green, who gave me information about the site for use in this book.

All Saints' church stands on a gentle slope looking south and west across the Pevensey Levels; it is about 2 miles south of the present village, close to the castle entrance. The church is dedicated to All Saints which is indicative of a Saxon origin and this is strengthened by the probability that standing on a rise it would be chosen as a place of worship in those times. The site may well be prehistoric as a sacred place. In the Domesday Book the Manor of Herste is mentioned and also 'there is a church'.

On the chancel floor, under a carpet, is an almost perfect brass to the memory

Telescopes in the domes.

of Sir William Fiennes (1402) whose son Sir Roger began to build the castle in the 1440s and whose grandson became the first Lord Dacre of this line. The brass represents a knight in pointed bascinet (Medieval European open-faced military helmet), camail (neck and shoulder covering of mail worn with and laced to the bascinet), mail shirt and armour, wearing a sword and a misericorde (long, narrow knife), with his feet resting on a lion.

The Dacre Chapel was added to the original church c.1450. The small chapel was given by the Fiennes family, who were then living at the castle, and is one of the earliest examples of brickwork in church buildings in Sussex. It contains the Gothic monument erected in 1534 to the memory of Thomas, 8th Lord Dacre (1470-1533) and his son Sir Thomas Fiennes who pre-deceased his father in 1528. The tomb is the main ornament in the church and is built of three types of

All Saints' church.

Dacre memorial tomb.

stone – Caen, Bonchurch and Purbeck marble. On the tomb lie the effigies of two men in Milanese armour, of about 1480 carved in Caen stone. Their hands are in an attitude of prayer and their feet on animals representing the Bull of the Dacres and the Alant (wolf hound) of the Fiennes.

Located near to Herstmonceux Castle and Observatory is the NERC, Space Geodesy Facility (SGF) which supports geodetic and geophysical science. It operates multiple observational techniques to make a major contribution to the formation of a highly-precise global geodetic reference frame and to support satellite missions that study the dynamic earth. The SGF makes range observations to enable orbit determination for scientific satellite missions that study the oceans, ice sheets, land mass, gravity field and climate of the Earth in order to better understand the processes at work. The site is passed on walk 12.

Now you can do the fairly easy walk to pass Herstmonceux Castle and visit the Observatory. I will see you back at the coast to explore Pevensey.

Sir William Fiennes brass (1402).

Space Geodesy Facility (SGF).

SUGGESTED WALK

WALK 12. Herstmonceux Observatory & Castle. (3.25 miles 5.2 km)

Parking. There is very limited roadside parking in Wartling Road in a layby next to the entrance to Herstmonceux Observatory and Castle. (Nearby postcode BN27 1RX.) The layby is generally only used by local walkers as the observatory and castle have their own large car parks; just check on-line that the observatory, in particular, is not having an 'events day' when it can become very busy and the layby will be full or try to start your walk early,

Herstmonceux Observatory.

ideally before 10a.m. The walk has been kept fairly short as the observatory is very popular with children as well as adults as they are fascinated by the telescopes and interactive attractions, so it can be visited after the walk. There are a few climbs, one stile and a few paths near the start can get muddy. Refreshments are available from the observatory which is worth visiting.

1. From the small layby go through the metal gate and diagonally right across a field on a feint grassy path with the observatory on your left. In the far corner go through a gap by a footpath sign into Plantation Wood. Go ahead with a wire fence on your left and descend gradually. Cross a stream and in a short distance, by a 3-way footpath sign, go left passing Snipe Pond on the right and Red Lily Pond on the left; the path in this area can get muddy after recent rain. Go through a gate and continue ahead to reach another gate; go through this gate to reach a 4-way footpath sign. Go left over the stile and ahead across a field heading for Herstmonceux Place which is in view ahead/slightly to the right. Continue until you go through a wide metal gate to reach a junction.

Herstmonceux Place.

Go left through a metal gate and along a wide track and in 20 yards go through another metal gate which has

Dacre memorial.

a 3-way footpath sign a few yards beyond it. Follow the grassy path between basic wire fences with a good view of Herstmonceux Place on your right. On the far side you reach Church Road, not signed. Go left up the quiet road and soon you reach All Saints' church on the right. The church contains the Dacre memorial tomb, Sir William Fiennes 1402 brass (which is under the carpet facing the altar), interesting stained-glass windows as well as other works of art; from the rear of the church grounds there are good views across the Pevensey Levels. The three wind turbines that you can see are at Shepham Wind Farm at Polegate. Seeing these wind turbines in this built-up area you can see how they are a benefit for the environment. The three turbines power 4888 homes annually, save c.7800 tonnes of CO_2 annually and have a 7.5mw capacity. As for the view you either love them or hate them.

2. Leave the church and continue along Church Road. In a few yards, by a 3-way footpath sign, go left along an access road. In a few yards go through a gate which is signposted with a '1066 Country Walk' sign beside the gate. Go along a concrete access road and at the end go through a metal gate (before you go through it go 10 yards to your left along the access road to reach the Space Geodesy Facility).

Follow the path down through trees and go through a gate. Go ahead across a field with views of Herstmonceux Castle on your left and in front of you is the top of the Newton Telescope which is now empty. (In 1979 the telescope was dismantled and completely refurbished before being installed on top of an extinct volcano on the Canary Island La Palma in 1984 where it operates with clearer skies.) Now just continue ahead going through gates and climbing up with a barbed-wire fence on your left. As you get near the top you get a good view of the observatory on your left. Continue ahead out to Watling Road and turn left past the entrance to the observatory and castle back to the layby. Now you can drive into the observatory car park to look at the telescopes and visit the castle if it is open.

Observatory telescope.

CHAPTER 10
PEVENSEY & PEVENSEY BAY

Pevensey is a village in the Wealden district of East Sussex. The main village is five miles (8 km) north-east of Eastbourne and it is one mile (1.6 km) inland from Pevensey Bay. The settlement of Pevensey Bay forms part of the parish and it was here that William the Conqueror landed in his invasion of England in 1066 after crossing the English Channel from Normandy.

Pevensey is situated on a spur of sand and clay, about 33 feet (10m) above sea level and in Roman times this spur was a peninsula that projected into a tidal lagoon and marshes. A small river called Pevensey Haven runs along the north side of the peninsula that would originally have discharged into the lagoon, but is now mainly silted up. The lagoon extended inland as far north as Hailsham and eastwards to Hooe but with the effect of longshore drift this large bay was gradually cut off from the sea by shingle, so that today's marshes are all that remain behind the shingle beach.

The marshes are known as Pevensey Levels and cover an area of around 47 square miles (122 km2). They are a Site of Special Scientific Interest and a large nature reserve which is jointly owned by Natural England and the Sussex Wildlife Trust. There are many nationally rare plants and invertebrates including the fen raft spider. The site is fragile and general access is not permitted.

Pevensey Bay lies behind and on the shingle beach. Although small it is still a seaside resort in miniature and has many of the facilities of its larger counterparts. It is a clay bay which makes it susceptible to erosion over time and the shingle beach provides an important defence against flooding and storm damage by the sea for a large area of low-lying land beyond.

The earliest evidence for the name Pevensey is in later charters dated 788 and 790 and names included Pefensea, Pæfensea and Pævenisel. The name means 'River of [a man named] Pefen' and derives from the Anglo-Saxon personal name Pefen plus eā, 'river', which may be a reference to the now largely silted-up Pevensey Haven.

In the sixteenth century Pevensey became a 'non-corporate limb' of the Hastings, as part of the Confederation of the Cinque Ports. Along with most of the other Ports, its importance dwindled as the ports themselves became disconnected from the sea.

During the eighteenth and nineteenth centuries Pevensey Bay became involved in the south coast smuggling trade as it was one of the easiest places to land the contraband. In 1833 a violent clash occurred between the smugglers and customs men at Pevensey Bay.

Pevensey Castle is a medieval castle and former Roman Saxon Shore fort and is a Scheduled Monument in the care of English Heritage. It was built c.290 AD and was known to the Romans as Anderitum and it appears to have been the base for a fleet called the Classis Anderidaensis.

Anderitum fell into ruin after the end of Roman occupation but was reoccupied in 1066 by the Normans for whom it became a key strategic rampart. A stone keep and fortification was built within the Roman walls and it faced several sieges but although its garrison was twice starved into surrender, it was never successfully stormed.

Pevensey Castle.

The castle was occupied almost continuously until the sixteenth century, apart from a possible break in the early thirteenth century when it was slighted (deliberate damage of high-status buildings to reduce their value as military, administrative or social structures) during the First Barons' War. It had been abandoned again by the late sixteenth century and remained a crumbling, partly overgrown ruin until it was acquired by the state in 1925.

The castle was reoccupied during WWII when it was garrisoned by units from the Home Guard, the British and Canadian armies and the United States Army Air Corps. Machine-gun posts were built into the Roman and medieval walls to control the flat land around Pevensey and defend against the threat of German invasion; they remain in place and can still be seen.

The castle covers an area of about 3.67 hectares (9.1 acres). It has an oval plan on a north-east/south-west alignment, that measures 290 metres (950 ft) by 170 metres (560 ft). It is the largest of the nine Saxon Shore forts and its walls and towers are the largest of any surviving Roman fort of the period. Its shape is unique among Saxon Shore forts and this was presumably determined by the contours of the peninsula on which it stands.

Courthouse Museum and Gaol.

Pevensey Courthouse Museum and Gaol (Jail) can be found along the High Street. Built in 1541 it remains as a slice of history with its Tudor beams still intact, it comprises a court room, prisoner's dock, magistrates' robing chamber and two prisoner's cells below with an exercise yard outside. It was within this small building with its intimidating iron-spiked walls that sentence was passed down to criminals; executions took place in Gallows Lane about half a mile down the road in Westham. This Grade II listed building was used as Pevensey's Gaol, Court and Tudor Town Hall up until 1886 when the borough was dissolved and it was the smallest Town Hall in England. There were a further six cells under the building which have now gone with the property attached being built for the Jailer c1700. Most of the old Pevensey Court House records were burnt in 1886 when it was dissolved but copies of all punishments meted out in England are also kept in London.

Today the Court House is a museum, where it houses a robing room and displayed there is the Great Seal of Charles I and the oldest surviving Cinque Port Seal c1230 which signified that Pevensey was a Cinque Port – one of a group of towns that pledged its supply of men and ships against invasion.

Ye Olde Mint House.

Along the High Street near the castle entrance and opposite the Royal Oak and Castle Inn is the Old Mint House (Ye Olde Mint House). The old half-timbered house is over 600 years old and has overhanging eaves and time-darkened red tiles. It is reputed to have been used as a Norman mint as far back as 1076. Built in 1342 to its present size and shape the interior was considerably altered in 1542 by Dr Andrew Borde who was then Court Physician to King Henry the Eighth. King Edward VI once stayed here for health benefits and the bedroom he used is still shown.

On the site of the present house was a building used since 1076 for minting coins and it is presumed to have been connected by an underground passage that ran beneath the Roman walls to the earliest part of the Norman castle. Coins were struck here during the reigns of William the Conqueror, William Rufus, Henry I and King Stephen between 1076 and 1154; it is believed that the mint ceased operations soon after the accession of Henry II. The mint is mentioned in the Domesday Book (1086) and four of the coins struck here are exhibited in the British Museum whilst a few others are scattered among provincial museums.

The Pevensey Levels is a low-lying area of agricultural land between Eastbourne and Bexhill-on-Sea that is one of the largest continuous lowland wet grazing systems in south east England. Despite extensive arable conversion, over 3500 ha (8649 acres) of grazing meadow still remain, intersected by a complex network of ditches. Aquatic communities supported by these ditches include 68% of British aquatic plant species and many nationally rare invertebrates. The national and international importance of the area is reflected in its designation as a SSSI and RAMSAR site. Some of the best habitat 181.6 ha (449 acres) is protected as a National Nature Reserve called Pevensey Marshes of which 130.2 ha (322 acres) is managed by the Sussex Wildlife Trust. The area may be the best in Britain

Pevensey Bay.

Martello Tower No. 60.

for freshwater mollusc fauna including the endangered shining rams-horn snail. It also has one nationally rare and several nationally scarce aquatic plants and it is of national importance for lapwing as it has more than 1% of the British population.

The Pevensey Bay area is home to three Martello Towers. The three towers are numbers 60 (Leyland Road), 61 (Millward Road) and 62 (Grey Tower Road).

Pevensey is also the starting point of the 31-mile 1066 Country Walk which is a long-distance footpath covering many historical sites in the area. The route commemorates the Battle of Hastings and links the places and people from that year. It runs through East Sussex from Pevensey where William of Normandy gathered his invading army of Normans and prepared to meet King Harold in Rye, passing through Battle. The walk is mainly low level and passes through ancient towns and villages, over hillsides and through woodland and passes oast houses (a building designed for kilning [drying] hops) and windmills. The route links with the Saxon Shore Way.

Martello Tower No. 62.

1066 Country Walk marker.

Now do walk 13 which starts by Pevensey Castle before passing Ye Old Mint House and Gaol before heading towards Pevensey Bay to pass three Martello Towers. The return route is across a section of Pevensey Levels. I will see you at Normans Bay and Bexhill, the home of British Motor Racing.

SUGGESTED WALK

WALK 13. Pevensey Castle, Pevensey Bay & 3 Martello Towers.
(4.5 miles 7.2 km)

Parking. Use the Castle Car Park at the junction of Castle Road and High Street. It is very close to the Castle entrance and is beside the Royal Oak & Castle Inn; the pub Post code is BN24 5LE. This is a level walk that takes you across the Pevensey Levels. There is one longish stretch beside a busy road but that is necessary so that we can visit all three of the Martello Towers in this area. The hardest bit is walking along the pebbled beach to reach Towers 61 and 62 and there are 3 stiles. Refreshments are available from the seafront area by Pevensey Bay and the Royal Oak & Castle Inn which is conveniently located at the start and finish.

1. From the car park go back to the High Street and go left through an arch into Pevensey Castle. Once you have explored the castle return back to the arch and go ahead along the High Street passing the Royal Oak & Castle Inn; Ye Old Mint House is directly opposite the pub. (It is over 600 years old and it is reputed to have been used as a Norman mint as long ago as 1076; in 1548 King Edward VI stayed for the benefit of his health). Continue along the road and you soon reach the Court House and Gaol on the right and the

Pevensey Castle.

long Smugglers pub on the left. Continue along the High Street until you reach a set of traffic lights. Turn right and go along Wallsend Road using the right-hand pavement (we need to walk down this busy road so that we can pass Martello Tower No. 60). Cross the railway line at Pevensey Bay station and continue to reach a set of traffic lights at Pevensey Bay. Turn right here and follow Richmond Road to its end where it meets the A259, Eastbourne Road. Cross over the A259 then go left down the second road which is Leyland Road and 40 yards down on your right is Martello Tower No. 60 which is an ideal example of how a Martello Tower can be converted and integrated into a residential home. Continue down Leyland Road to reach the beach at the end at Pevensey Bay – no more roads.

Royal Oak and Castle Inn.

2. Now turn right and walk along the beach heading for Towers 61 and 62; in the distance you can clearly make out Martello Tower No. 66 which is at the east breakwater at Sovereign Harbour, Eastbourne, which you visited on walk 11. As you walk along the beach keep a look out on your right as Tower 61 just appears; it only sits back a short distance from the beach and is easy to see but you can't see it until you are beside it. Continue until you reach Tower 62 which is much easier to see but more difficult to photograph as it is surrounded by caravans at Grey Tower Caravan Park.

Martello Tower No. 61.

3. Turn right and go along the road to the right of Tower 62, through the caravan park, and at its end you reach the A259. Cross over, go 10 yards to the right then go over a stile in the hedgerow by a footpath sign. Go across a field on a faint grassy path aiming for a footpath sign, in sight, which is at the start of some hedgerow on the right-hand side. Follow a meandering grassy path and soon you will be walking with a wire fence on your right. At a junction go left over a substantial bridge and continue with a barbed-wire fence on your left. (By the way you are now on the Pevensey Levels with all its drainage ditches so look out for its butterflies and other wildlife). Cross a metal bridge and continue ahead for 20 yards then go left and head across a field on a grassy path which soon curves left beside a ditch. Aim for a marker post ahead at the end of a row of trees. Go through a gap in the hedgerow and diagonally left to a stile in the far left-hand corner.

Castle ruin from footpath.

Go over the stile and cross a railway line. Cross another stile then go left along a left field edge. At a junction go left over a bridge and ahead along the left-hand side of a graveyard. At the end of the graveyard, you will see the church of St Mary at Westham to the left which you can visit if you wish but to continue the walk you turn right here and follow the path soon with limited views of the castle on your left. Just keep going until you arrive back at the car park.

CHAPTER 11
NORMANS BAY & BEXHILL

Normans Bay is a coastal hamlet in the Pevensey Levels area and contrary to popular belief it does not take its name from the Norman Conquests of 1066; the forces of William the Conqueror are believed to have landed at nearby Pevensey.

The hamlet is surrounded by mostly dry marshland to the north in which lay the land remains of an ancient settlement known as Northeye. The deserted village is situated in an area called Hooe Level which is part of the Pevensey Levels – a lowland marsh area between Bexhill and Eastbourne. Originally most of the Pevensey Levels would have been submerged at high tide and the settlements would have been on small islands (eyots). The village is mentioned as a dependent limb of the Cinque Port of Hastings in a charter of 1229. It is thought to have been deserted around 1400 and it consisted of houses and a flint-built chapel, the Chapel of St James.

The Domesday Book records that the edges of Pevensey Marsh supported 100 salt works which suggests that at that time salt water still flooded much of the area and several mounds near the village suggest that this may well have played a role in the economy of Northeye.

Normans Bay.

Martello Tower No. 55 is located on the beach at Normans Bay and it has retained many of its original components. During the nineteenth century it became one of four Martello towers to be fitted with a semaphore machine and in the early 1900s it was used for a series of wireless telegraphy experiments. The tower was converted to a Battery Observation Post during WWII. After WWII it was left empty until it was sold to a private buyer in 2004 who converted it into a private residence. The tower is passed on walk 14.

Martello Tower No. 55.

103

In 2005 divers who were trying to free a lobster pot discovered a large anchor and cannons offshore. Originally it was thought to be the remains of the English warship HMS *Resolution* which sunk there in 1703 but ongoing research suggests the wreck might be the Dutch warship *Wapen van Utrecht* which sank during the Battle of Beachy Head in 1690.

The Star Inn.

The Star Inn was formerly a sluice house and became an inn around the time of the civil war. It is likely to have got its name 'star' because it was frequented by shepherds and was known as 'The Star of Bethlehem' which was eventually shortened to 'The Star'.

In the eighteenth century organised smugglers using wooden clubs and poles fought customs men with cutlasses in front of The Star. The local gang were led and organised by a local family from nearby Little Common. They numbered about thirty resolute men and records show that they owned two boats, the *Queen Charlotte*, named after the wife of George III and *The Long Boat*; both of these boats were kept at a spot known locally as *Willow Tot* in front of the then lonely Star Inn. They were big boats that were capable of bringing hundreds of tubs of contraband brandy from France. We visit the Star Inn on walk 14.

BEXHILL

Bexhill or Bexhill-on-Sea is a seaside town to the west of Hastings. The ancient town is home to a number of archaeological sites, a manor house in the Old Town and has an abundance of Edwardian and Victorian architecture.

The first reference to Bexhill to Bexelei as it was originally called, was in a charter granted by King Offa of Mercia in 772 AD. It is recorded that King Offa had 'defeated the men of Hastings' in 771 AD; at this time the term Hastings would have referred to this whole area rather than the town itself. In the charter King Offa established a church and religious community in Bexhill.

During the Norman Conquest of 1066 Bexhill was largely destroyed and the Domesday survey of 1086 records that the manor was worth £20 before the conquest, was 'waste' in 1066 and was worth £18 10s in 1086. King William I used the lands he had conquered to reward his knights and he gave Bexhill Manor to Robert, Count of Eu, as well as most of the Hastings area. Robert's grandson John, Count of Eu, gave the manor back to the bishops of Chichester in 1148 and it is likely that the first manor house was built by the bishops at this time. The later manor house, the ruins of which can still be seen at the Manor Gardens in Bexhill

Old Town, was built around 1250 probably on the instructions of St Richard, bishop of Chichester. Richard of Wych was the 9th bishop of Chichester and the most famous visitor at this time who had a close association with the ancient parish. The destructive power of a great storm in 1250 can still be seen today with the petrified remains of the submerged wood to the east of Galley Hill. In 1276 a large portion of Bexhill was made into a park for hunting. The oldest remains of the manor house date from this time which leads to speculation that Richard of Wych had part of the residence rebuilt following the storm damage; and it is also believed that it was on a journey from the Bishop's Palace to Dover that he died in 1253. Nine years after his death Richard was canonised and as St Richard, he was later made the patron saint of Sussex. In 1447 Bishop Adam de Moleyns was given permission to fortify the manor house.

Manor house ruins.

In 1561 Queen Elizabeth I took possession of Bexhill Manor and three years later she gave it to Sir Thomas Sackville, Earl of Dorset; the Earls, later Dukes, of Dorset owned Bexhill until the mid-nineteenth century.

In 1804 soldiers of the King's German Legion were stationed in barracks at Bexhill; they were Hanoverians who had escaped when their country was overrun by Napoleon's army. As King George III was also the Elector of Hanover, he welcomed them and they fought as part of the British Army and it was about this time that the defensive Martello Towers were built along the south east coast, some close to Bexhill. In 1814 the soldiers of the King's German Legion left Bexhill eventually playing a major part in the Battle of Waterloo the following year.

In 1813 Elizabeth Sackville had married the 5th Earl De La Warr and when the male line of the Dukes of Dorset died out in 1865, she and her husband inherited Bexhill. It was the 7th Earl De La Warr who decided to transform the small rural village of Bexhill into an exclusive seaside resort. He contracted builder John Webb to construct the first sea wall and to lay out De La Warr Parade. In part payment for his work, Webb was given all the land from Sea Road to the Polegrove, south of the railway line. Opened in 1890 the Sackville Hotel was built for the 7th Earl De La Warr and it originally included a house for family use. In 1891 Viscount Cantelupe, his eldest surviving son married Muriel Brassey the daughter of Sir Thomas, later Earl Brassey, and the late Anna, Lady Brassey of Normanhurst Court near Bexhill. The Manor House was fully refurbished so that Lord and Lady Cantelupe could live in style as Lord and Lady of the Manor. Finally, the 7th Earl de La Warr transferred control of his Bexhill estate to Viscount Cantelupe when he died in 1896.

Viscount Cantelupe became the 8th Earl De La Warr and it was at this time that he organised the building on the sea front of the Kursaal, a pavilion for refined entertainment and relaxation. In 1902 Bexhill became an Incorporated Borough. This was the first Royal Charter granted by Edward VII; Bexhill was the last town in Sussex to be incorporated and it was the first time that a Royal Charter was delivered by motorcar. To celebrate the town's newfound status the 8th Earl De La Warr organised the country's first ever motorcar races along De La Warr Parade in May 1902. This was in conjunction with the Automobile Club of Britain and Ireland which later became the RAC. The Sackville Hotel which still stands today (Sackville Apartments) was their headquarters for the races which continued in Bexhill until the first purpose-built track was opened at Brooklands in 1907.

At this time the town was scandalised by the divorce of Earl De La Warr. Muriel had bought the action on the grounds of adultery and abandonment; she was granted a divorce and given custody of their three children. Muriel and her children went back to live with Earl Brassey at Normanhurst Court and the 8th Earl De La Warr remarried but was again divorced for adultery. At the start of WWI, the Earl bought a Royal Naval commission; he died of fever at Messina in 1915.

Sackville Apartments.

Birthplace of British Motor Racing.

Herbrand Edward Dundonald Brassey Sackville became the 9th Earl De La Warr and he is best known for championing the construction of the De La Warr Pavilion which was built and opened in 1935. He also became Bexhill's first socialist Mayor and died in 1976.

The most noticeable building in Bexhill-on-Sea is the De La Warr Pavilion which is a Grade I listed building on the seafront. It was the result of an architectural competition started by Herbrand Sackville the 9th Earl De La Warr after whom the building is named. He persuaded Bexhill council to develop the site as a public building and the competition was announced in *The Architects' Journal* in February 1934 specifying that it required an entertainment hall to seat at least 1500 people, a 200-seat restaurant, a reading room and a lounge. The initial budget was £50,000 but it was later increased to £80,000. Run by the Royal Institute of British Architects the competition attracted over 230 entrants many of them practicing in the Modernist style. The architects selected were Erich Mendelsohn and Serge Chermayeff who were leading figures in the Modern Movement.

The aesthetics used in the International Style proved well suited to the building, tending towards streamlined, industrially-influenced designs, often with expansive metal-framed windows and excluded the traditional brick and stonework in favour of concrete and steel construction. Among the building's most innovative features was its welded steel frame construction which was pioneered by structural engineer Felix Samuely; construction began in January 1935. The Pavilion was opened on 12 December of the same year by the Duke and Duchess of York (later King George VI and Queen Elizabeth).

During WWII the Pavilion was used by the military. Bexhill was vulnerable if the Germans decided to invade and amongst those who served at the Pavilion during the war was Terence Alan Milligan better known as Spike Milligan who later became a noted comedian and one of the Goons. The building suffered minor damage to its foundations when the Metropole Hotel adjacent to the building's western side was destroyed by German bombers.

After the war management of the Pavilion was taken over by Bexhill Corporation (later Rother District Council) and changes were made to the building which were not in keeping with the original design or aesthetics of the building. A lack of funds also resulted in an ongoing degradation of the building's fabric. In 1986 the Pavilion was granted Grade I listed building status which protected it from any further inappropriate alteration. 1989 saw the formation of the Pavilion Trust a group dedicated to protecting and restoring the building. Playwright David Hare suggested that the site be used as an art gallery as opposed to an expected privatised redevelopment. In 2002 after a lengthy application process the Pavilion was granted £6 Million by the Heritage Lottery Fund & the Arts Council to restore the building and turn it into a contemporary arts centre. Work began in 2004 on its regeneration and transfer of the building's ownership went from Rother District Council to the De La Warr Pavilion Charitable Trust. In 2005 after extensive restoration and regeneration the Pavilion reopened as a contemporary arts centre, encompassing one of the largest galleries on the south coast of England.

De La Warr Pavilion.

Wreck of VOC *Amsterdam* (at 1.0m tide).   4000-year-old sunken forest.

The Pavilion has featured works by Andy Warhol, Cerith Wyn Evans and Richard Wilson amongst others and in July 1972 Bob Marley had his first ever UK gig here when he appeared as support for Johnny Nash who had a big hit with 'I can See Clearly Now'; the event was organised by Bexhill Lions Club to raise money for the Glyne Gap swimming pool fund. Performances since have included Elvis Costello, Goldfrapp, Ray Davies, Years and Years, Patti Smith and Laurie Anderson.

A Site of Special Scientific Interest lies within the Bexhill district; known as High Woods which is just north of Little Common. It is of biological importance because it is the only known sessile oak woodland in East Sussex. Fossils are also commonly found in Bexhill and in 2009 the world's oldest spider's web was found encased in amber in the town; it was 140 million years old. In June 2011 it was reported that the world's smallest dinosaur had been discovered at Ashdown Brickworks near the town when a single vertebra was found.

The wreck of the VOC *Amsterdam*, an eighteenth century cargo ship that ran aground between Bexhill and St Leonards can be seen at low tide. From the main A259 it is opposite Bridge Way and can only be seen at very low tides (try to get a tide below 1.0m). In the same place as the shipwreck is a 4000-year-old submerged forest which is also revealed at low tide. When the trees were growing the sea levels were much lower and the coastline was further out; there is an information board directly opposite.

Bexhill Clock Tower, located on the seafront by the junction with Park Avenue, was originally intended to commemorate the coronation of King Edward VII in 1902 but it was not completed until 1904. It was designed by Robert Hembrow and was built by local builders Benjamin Gaston and F. Ransome. It stands some 27.5 ft high (8.4 m) with a single stepped base and is made from imitation Bath stone. It has an entrance door on the north side, clock faces on all four sides and a weather vane on top.

Now you can do the associated walks to visit Martello Tower No. 55 and the Star Inn at Normans Bay and the De La Warr Pavilion, manor house ruins and the birthplace of British Motor Racing at Bexhill-on-Sea. I will see you further inland for our next visit which is to the lovely Bodiam Castle and a steam railway.

SUGGESTED WALK

WALK 14. Normans Bay, Martello Tower No. 55 and Star Inn
(4.75 miles 7.6 km)

Parking. There is a free car park along The Gorses (Post Code TN39 3BE). If full there is limited roadside parking or parking along the top of the beach in Herbrand Walk just past the beach huts and start the walk at Section 2. This is a fairly easy walk along the beach and lanes and there are no stiles. Refreshments are available from the Star Inn.

1. From the car park go left along The Gorses then go left down Cooden Sea Road using the right-hand pavement. Go under the railway and continue to reach the beach at the end passing Cooden Beach Hotel on the right. Turn right along the beach and aim for Martello Tower No. 55 which is in view at Normans Bay. Soon you reach a row of beach huts where cars do park on busy days and which can be used as an alternative starting point for this walk.

2. From the beach huts walk along the beach (or take your shoes off, roll up your trousers and paddle) and head towards the Martello Tower; the pebbles are quite small and compact so walking on the beach is quite easy here. (Ahead you have views past Pevensey to Eastbourne.)

3. From the tower return back along the beach for 30 yards then go left out to Coast Road, not signed. Go right along the fairly quiet road and follow it around to the left passing Normans Bay Caravan Park on the right. Cross the railway line at Normans Bay Station and continue up the road and in a few yards turn right and walk along the road beside the Pevensey Levels. Soon you reach the Star Inn on the left (once famous for smuggling) for welcome refreshments.

Beach huts at Cooden Beach.

4. Leave the pub, go left over a bridge and continue to follow the road as it soon curves to the right and re-crosses the railway line. Soon you arrive back at the beach where you go left along your outward route back to the start.

Martello Tower No. 55.

SUGGESTED WALK

WALK 15. De La Warr Pavilion, Sackville Hotel, manor house ruins, Egerton Park and Bexhill Clock Tower. (3.25 miles 5.2 km)

Parking. Park in the De La Warr Pavilion car park (Post Code TN40 1DP) or nearby; or arrive by bus or train. This is a short, fairly easy walk with a gradual climb near the start on the way to the manor house ruins; there are no stiles. Refreshments are available throughout the walk at pubs, shops etc.

1. From wherever you park the walk starts by the beach facing the De La Warr Pavilion. After exploring and photographing the Pavilion head east along the beachfront path with the sea on your right and Hastings in view ahead which you will visit in Chapter 13. Go to the end of the path and then go left up to the main road. Turn right soon passing a war memorial and a plaque marking the 'Finishing Line 1902 for the First International Motor Race Meeting in Great Britain'. Cross over the main road here and go right to reach the Sackville Hotel with its blue plaque showing its claim to fame as the 'Birthplace of British Motor Racing'

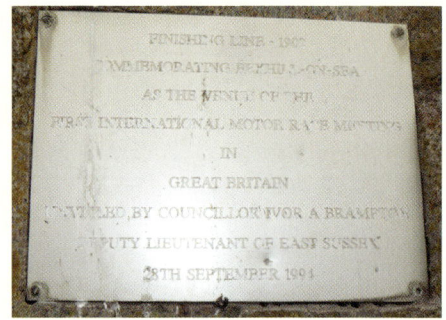
Finishing Line 1902 plaque.

2. Immediately after the Sackville Hotel go left up the next side road and just keep going climbing gradually and crossing a railway line. Continue ahead up Manor Road and at the top go left along De La Warr Road, not signed. In about 150 yards go left into the car park for Manor House Barn and Gardens. (The access to the gardens is to the left

Sackville Hotel and blue plaque.

of the public toilets but the main ruins are actually a little further past the car park near the road. It is worth exploring the whole area).

3. Leave by the same entrance or by the ruins and continue left along De La Warr Road for a few yards and at a road junction go left down Upper Sea Road soon passing De Moleyns Close on your left. Just follow the road down passing St Mary Magdalene's church and just past it cross over the road and go right along the road to the left of Bexhill train station. Follow the road and continue ahead up

Manor House Barn and Gardens.

Manor house ruins.

a one-way road passing shops and where you can take refreshments (or get your nails done).

Cross a set of traffic lights and continue ahead along the left-hand pavement. Soon you reach Park Road with the entrance to Egerton Park beside it. Enter the park and walk to the right of the of the pond following the watercourse all the way to its end by Bexhill Museum. Turn left at the museum and just past it go right up a ramp to reach a road. Go right along the road for 40 yards then go left down Park Avenue to reach Bexhill Clock Tower. Turn left along the road back to the Pavilion in sight.

Egerton Park Pond.

Bexhill Clock Tower.

CHAPTER 12
BODIAM

Bodiam is a small village that lies in the valley of the River Rother near to the villages of Sandhurst and Ewhurst Green. The village dates to Roman times when a settlement and port were established for ships that came to trade for Sussex iron and the Roman road from Hastings to Rochester crossed at this point. After the Romans' departure the area was occupied by the Anglo-Saxons who it is believed gave the place its original name of 'Bodan Hamm'. However, it was the medieval period which had the greatest impact on the area as the most outstanding feature of Bodiam is its moated ruined castle which was built in the reign of Richard II between 1385 and 1390.

In 1946 nearly 1200 acres of land in and around Bodiam were leased to the Guinness family for hops to be grown and around 2000 people travelled yearly from London and further afield to pick the hops. By 1976 the introduction of mechanical aids meant that hand picking the hops was no longer required. The railway which brought many of the pickers to Bodiam was closed in 1961 but it has been restored and the Kent and East Sussex Railway from Tenterden to Bodiam is a popular tourist attraction and makes an ideal route to Bodiam Castle.

On 15 May 1919, a South Eastern & Chatham Railway Van left Dover on its way to London carrying a very important passenger; her name was Edith Cavell and after a long war she was finally being brought home to be laid to rest. Edith Cavell was an English nurse working in Belgium at a Red Cross hospital during WWI. Between 1914 and when she was arrested on the 5 August 1915, she had helped over 200 allied soldiers to escape. She was shot by a German firing squad in Brussels on 12 October 1915 at the age of forty-nine. After the war, following her journey home from Dover to London railway vans of the same type became known as 'Cavells'; a state funeral was held in her honour. The fully restored railway van now sits in a siding at the rear of Bodiam Station and inside a single coffin sits in the centre as a reminder of the cost of war. An inscription on the coffin reads: A British warrior who fell in the great war of 1914-1918 for king and country.

The coffin is a replica of the one that carried the body of the Unknown Warrior. It has been built by volunteers

Kent and East Sussex Railway.

from the Kent and East Sussex Railway using elm wood from the Royal Parks. The metal work holds a poignant link to the past. (Full information relating to the 'Cavell Van' No. 132 and its history is available inside the van.

The Kent and East Sussex Railway (K&SR) is now 10.5 miles long and is a fine example of one of England's light railways that was originally part of a larger system which operated between Headcorn and Robertsbridge. The K&SR was the very first 'light railway' to be constructed: light railways are equipped with full size trains but have steep gradients and operate at low speed.

Passenger trains ran from 1900 until 1954. A scheme to reopen the railway was proposed but it was not until 1974 that the first trains were able to run on a short section of line. The registered charity that now owns and operates

'Cavell Van' and coffin.

the line was able to finally restore services to Bodiam in time for the centenary of the line in 2000 and today it welcomes around 90,000 people a year.

Some of the trains are approaching 150 years old and the journey time between Tenterden and Bodiam is around fifty minutes each way. Some of the trains include carriages with old-fashioned family compartments and a Freedom Ticket allows you to hop on and off any of the trains that are operating on the day of your visit.

South of the village and extending to the railway station is the site of a Roman settlement that was investigated in the 1960s. The site was located within the land of the former Guinness hop gardens and the excavations were undertaken between the rows of hops. A comprehensive landscape survey was carried out around 2016.

The Castle Inn was formerly known as The Red Lion until it was rebuilt in 1885 and renamed. Its story is linked to the castle and it probably came into being in the fifteenth century when merchants and tradesmen came on business to the castle. The inn provided the only accommodation for visitors to Bodiam and also catered for canal traffic which used to reach the nearby bridge.

The parish church of St Giles is in a picturesque setting half a mile to the north of the castle and is a much-restored fourteenth century building. Inside there is a brass of a knight and the arms of the Bodeham family. A former rector of the church was once aide-de-camp (personal assistant or secretary to a person of high rank) to the Ethiopian emperor Haile Selassie and one of the six bells in the tower is named after him.

The famous artist J. M. W. Turner was a visitor to Bodiam and he painted the castle and bridge over the River Rother.

Bodiam Castle is a fourteenth century moated castle with the castle sitting roughly in the middle of the moat. It was built in 1385 by Sir Edward Dalyngrigge a former knight of Edward III, with the permission of Richard II, to defend the area against the French in the Hundred Years' War. It is of a quadrangular plan with no keep, having its chambers built around the outer defensive walls and inner courts. Its corners and entrance are marked by towers and topped with crenellations (gaps at regular intervals for firing arrows). The castle's structure, details and its location in an artificial watery landscape, show that display was an important part of the castle's design as well as defence. It was the home of the Dalyngrigge family and the centre of the manor of Bodiam.

Possession of the castle passed through several generations of Dalyngrigges until their line became extinct and the castle passed by marriage to the Lewknor family. During the Wars of the Roses, Sir Thomas Lewknor supported the House of Lancaster and when Richard III of the House of York became king in 1483, a force was despatched to besiege Bodiam Castle. It is not recorded if the siege went ahead but it is thought that Bodiam was surrendered without much resistance. The castle was confiscated but returned to the Lewknors when Henry VII of the House of Lancaster became king in 1485. Descendants of the Lewknors owned the castle until at least the sixteenth century.

By the start of the English Civil war in 1641, Bodiam Castle was in the possession of Lord Thanet. He supported the Royalist cause and sold the castle to help pay fines levied against him by Parliament. The castle was subsequently dismantled and was left as a picturesque ruin until its purchase by John Fuller in

Bodiam Castle.

1829 ('Mad Jack' Fuller or as he preferred to be known 'Honest John' Fuller; who amongst other things was a builder of follies). Under his guidance the castle was partially restored before being sold to George Cubitt, 1st Baron Ashcombe and later to Lord Curzon, both of whom undertook further restoration work. The castle is a Grade I listed building and Scheduled Monument. It has been owned by The National Trust since 1925, donated by Lord Curzon on his death and is open to the public.

Coats of arms above the castle gate.

Just above the gate there are three coats of arms carved in relief into the arch; left to right they are the arms of the Wardeux, Dalyngrigge and Radynden families. The Wardeux family was that of Edward Dalyngrigge's wife and the Radyndens were relations of the Dalyngrigges; above the arms is a unicorn head crest. Although the exterior of the castle has largely survived the interior is ruinous. The domestic buildings within the castle lined the curtain walls. However, the remains are substantial enough to recreate a plan of the castle.

The castle's location was supposedly chosen to protect England's south coast from raids by the French. A landscape survey by the Royal Commission for Historic Monuments concluded that if this were the case, then Bodiam Castle was unusually sited as it is far from the medieval coast. (However, I feel it does justify its inclusion in this book – especially as it is my favourite castle.)

Bodiam Castle was used in *Monty Python and the Holy Grail* 1975, in an establishing shot identifying it as 'Swamp Castle' in the 'Tale of Sir Lancelot' sequence. Previously it had been used for the filming of 'Camelot', an episode of *The Goodies* in 1973. Later it was used as the filming location for the Doctor Who serial *The King's Demons* in 1983.

Now you can do the associated walk to visit Bodiam Castle and if you time it right you can combine it to see a steam train at Bodiam Station; see their website for the train times. I will see you back at the coast to continue the journey at St Leonards-on-Sea and Hastings for the mummified cats.

Unicorn head crest.

SUGGESTED WALK

WALK 16. Bodiam Castle. (5.75 miles 9.3 km)

Parking. There is roadside parking by St James the Great church (Post code TN32 5TD). This is a fairly easy walk with a few gradual climbs but there are 13 stiles. Refreshments are available from the White Dog pub at the start/finish, the Tea Room at Bodiam Castle and the Castle Inn opposite the castle. PLEASE NOTE: If you plan your visit correctly you can combine your castle visit with a ride, or just viewing, of the steam train at Bodiam Station; it runs between Bodiam and Tenterden. Check the kesr.org.uk website for their timetable.

1. With your back to the church of St James the Great go left along the road passing the village sign for Ewhurst Green. (Refreshments were available from the White Dog pub 25 yards along the road to the right.) Walk along the quiet road using the right-hand pavement and very soon by a swing gate on your right you get your first view of Bodiam Castle in the distance. (This is where you return.) Continue along the road, taking extra care when the pavement ends, to reach a road junction at Dagg Lane.

Bodiam Castle.

Trebuchet.

Ahead, to the right of the road sign for Dagg Lane, cross the stile to the right of a wide gate. Go diagonally right along a faint grassy path and cross a stile in the far-right corner. Go through woodland, cross a bridge and continue to reach an access track. Cross a stile opposite and go ahead through a gate in a wire fence. Continue directly ahead across the next field and descend to a stile (you have to go into the left-hand edge of trees) and go out to a lane.

Go right down the lane and in 20 yards go left along an access drive and almost immediately go right over a stile to the left of a wide gate. Go ahead down a left field edge with a house on your right and cross another stile. Cross a bridge and continue on a slightly overgrown path which soon continues through trees. Cross a bridge and in a few yards at a junction go left up to a field. Turn right and walk along the right field edge and soon you continue ahead along an access road. At the end of the access road go left for 15 yards then go right out to an access track. Go ahead to a stile to the left of a building and go right down an enclosed right field edge. At the bottom go right through a swing gate and continue down a driveway to reach a road via a gate that is a few yards over to your right.

2. Turn right and with care walk along the road and cross the bridge in sight. Immediately after the bridge go right and follow the riverside path. After about a mile you reach a bridge. Go up to the road (Bodiam Station is to the right in view) and go left to reach the Castle Inn on your left for a beer or wine or the Tea Shop on your right for a tea or coffee (I know which one I prefer). Turn right past the Tea Room to reach Bodiam Castle.

3. Once you have explored the castle return to the main entrance by the Castle Inn. Go left and 25 yards after the bridge go left at a footpath sign. (Ahead of you down the road you can see Bodiam train station with its carriages. The Kent and East Sussex Railway operate a very popular steam train services between Tenterden and Bodiam and if you have planned your visit correctly you can go to the station to see the trains even if you decide not to ride the train. Also at the station is the 'Cavell Van').

Steam train at Bodiam Station.   'Cavell Van'.

Go left and walk along the raised bank close to the river. Just before a gate go right at a marker post and walk with a wire fence on your left. In the corner go right and in about 75 yards go left over a stile and cross the railway line. Cross a stile on the other side and go left over another stile then go right to cross a bridge in view. Go ahead up a right field edge and in the far corner go over a bridge/stile then go ahead to a 3-way footpath sign in sight to the left of a gate. Go ahead (not right) up across the field and cross a stile in the far corner. Follow the left edge of the next field and cross a stile to the left of a gate. Go through a swing gate then go right up a right field edge. At the top go through a swing gate and left along the road back to the start.

If any of you are wondering what the houses are with white angled tops, they are oast houses. They are buildings designed for kilning (drying) hops as part of the brewing process and are particularly popular in Kent and Sussex.

CHAPTER 13
ST LEONARDS-ON-SEA & HASTINGS

St Leonards-on-Sea which is usually just referred to as St Leonards is a town and seaside resort to the west of its larger neighbour Hastings. The original part of the town was laid out in the nineteenth century as a new town with elegant houses for the rich and included a central public garden, hotel, an archway, assembly rooms and a church. St Leonards has grown well beyond the original design but the old town still exists within it.

The land that is now St Leonards was once owned by the Levett family who were an ancient Sussex gentry family of Norman origin who also owned the adjacent manor of Hollington and then by their descendants the Eversfields who rose to prominence from their iron foundries and property holdings during Tudor times. The Eversfields served as sheriffs of Surrey and Sussex in the sixteenth and seventeenth centuries and were later baronets before the family became extinct.

James Burton who was a London property developer who had developed large areas of Bloomsbury and the houses around Regent's Park purchased land from the Eversfield estate to use in his plan for a seaside resort. The land was part of Gensing Farm and included a small wooded valley leading down to the sea. Work on the plan started in early 1826 and it included a house for himself. Service areas were provided such as shops and laundering as well as public buildings for entertainment and the picturesque siting of villas amongst the wooded slopes to be paid for by subscription.

Before his death in 1837 the Royal Victoria Hotel, South Colonnade (an archway marking the town boundary with Hastings – demolished in 1929) and tall seafront houses as far as 71 Marina had all been completed. His grave is marked by a

James Burton's grave (now fenced off due to cliff erosion).

Royal Victoria Hotel.

pyramid in the churchyard above St Leonard's church. In 1850 his son Decimus began the second phase of building by acquiring more land and extending the development westwards, he lived in the town for the rest of his life. Queen Victoria stayed at the Victoria Hotel.

St Leonards became a fashionable seaside destination and Princess Sophia of Gloucester stayed at Gloucester Lodge on Quarry Hill in 1831; the building was formerly named Castellated Villa but was changed in her honour. Princess Victoria and her mother the Duchess of Kent stayed in the town for the winter of 1834-5 at a residence since renamed Victoria House, then Crown House. In 1837 Queen Adelaide passed the winter there.

The popularity of St Leonards was not lost upon the neighbouring town of Hastings who began to expand westwards. The Eversfield Estate from whom the Burtons had bought land saw the potential and it too began to sell off more space having obtained an Act of Parliament opening the way for speculative builders beyond the Burton boundaries. As a result, the area between the two towns began to fill with properties and in 1875 the two towns merged into the County Borough of Hastings and by then the total seafront had reached three miles (4.8 km). Soon after the Warrior Square and Upper St Leonards areas were being developed.

Marine Court.

On the seafront there is an ocean liner shaped art-deco building called Marine Court which when completed in 1937 was the tallest block of flats in the UK, comprising 153 flats and three restaurants. Despite its claim to fame entries for a competition to name the building show that it was not universally popular but it is now a listed building. The building can be seen all along the seafront and is a local landmark.

HASTINGS

Hastings is a seaside town that gives its name to the Battle of Hastings (14 October 1066) which took place 8 miles (13 km) to the north-west at Senlac Hill. It later became one of the Cinque Ports and in the nineteenth century it was a popular seaside resort as the railway enabled tourists and visitors to reach the town. Today Hastings is a fishing port with the UK's largest beach-based fishing fleet.

The first mention of Hastings is in the eighth century as Hastingas which is derived from the Old English tribal name Hæstingas meaning 'the followers of Hæsta'. Symeon of Durham records the victory of Offa in 771 over the Hestingorum gens 'the people of the Hastings tribe'.

Evidence of prehistoric settlements have been found at the town site and flint arrowheads and Bronze Age artefacts have also been found. Iron Age forts have been excavated on both East and West Hills. The settlement was already based on the port when the Romans arrived in Britain in 55 BC and at this time, they began to exploit the iron (Wealden rocks contain a plentiful supply of the ore) and shipped it out by boat. Iron was worked locally at Beauport Park to the north of the town; it employed up to one thousand men and is thought to be the third-largest mine in the Roman Empire.

When the Romans left the town suffered setbacks, the Beauport site was abandoned and the town suffered problems from nature and man-made attacks. The Sussex coast has always suffered from occasional violent storms and with the hazard of longshore drift (the eastward movement of shingle along the coast) the coastline has frequently changed; the original Roman port is now probably under the sea.

Hastings looking east towards the Country Park.

Hastings was shown as a borough by the time of the Domesday Book of 1086 and it had given its name to the Rape of Hastings, one of the six administrative divisions of Sussex. Muslim scholar Muhammad al-Idrisi writing c.1153 described Hastings as 'a town of large extent and many inhabitants, flourishing and handsome, having markets, workpeople and rich merchants'.

Fish smoking huts.

ST LEONARDS-ON-SEA & HASTINGS

 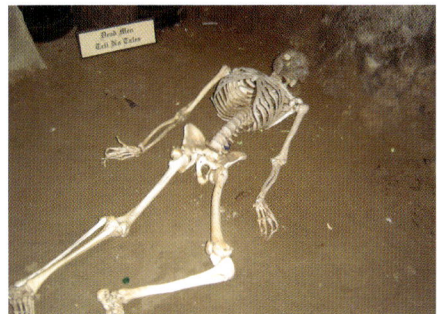

St Clements Cave – 'Smugglers Adventure'.

In the thirteenth century much of the town and half of Hastings Castle was washed away in the South England Flood of February 1287. During a naval campaign of 1339 and again in 1377 the town was raided and burnt by the French and went into decline so as a port Hastings was finished. Hastings has suffered over the years from the lack of a natural harbour and there have been attempts to create a sheltered harbour. An attempt to build a stone harbour was made during the reign of Elizabeth I but the foundations were destroyed by the sea during a bad storm; the fishing boats are still stored and launched from the beach.

At that time Hastings was a small fishing settlement but it was soon discovered that the new taxes on luxury goods could be made profitable by smuggling and the town was ideally located for that purpose. Near the castle ruins on West Hill are St Clements Caves, partly natural but mainly excavated by hand by smugglers from the soft sandstone. Their trade came to an end with the period following the Napoleonic Wars as the town became one of the most fashionable resorts in Britain, brought about by the health-giving properties of seawater as well as the local springs and Roman baths. The caves were named after a nearby church and since 1989 are home to 'Smugglers Adventure' a tourist attraction which tells the story of smuggling on the south coast of England 200 years ago.

Hastings is located where the sandstone beds at the heart of the Weald, known geologically as the Hastings Sands, meet the English Channel, forming tall cliffs to the east of the town. Hastings Old Town is in a sheltered valley between East Hill and West Hill, on which the remains of the castle stand. The sandstone cliffs have been subjected to considerable erosion in recent times and much of the castle was lost to the sea before the present sea defences and promenade were built. The beach is mainly shingle with wide areas of sand exposed at low tide.

Hastings Castle was built in 1070 by the Normans, four years after the Norman invasion. It is a keep and bailey castle ruin on West Hill that overlooks the English Channel into which large parts of the castle have fallen into over the years. It is a Grade I listed building but little remains of the castle apart from the arch left from the chapel, part of the walls and dungeons. In 1287 violent storms battered the south coast for many months and the soft sandstone cliffs eventually succumbed

Hastings Castle.

to the elements when large sections of the cliffs fell into the sea along with parts of the castle. Throughout the following century erosion was unchecked and gradually more of the castle was lost to the sea. The site was purchased by Thomas Pelham on 23 June 1591 and after the purchase the Pelham family used the site for farming until the ruins had become so overgrown, they were lost from memory. In 1824 the then owner, the Earl of Chichester, commissioned some archaeological investigations of the ruin. As a result, the chapel floor and parts of the chancel arch and walls were re-constructed out of blocks found lying on the ground.

During WWII the castle received more damage as Hastings was a target for bombing raids. In 1951 the Hastings Corporation purchased the site and converted it into a tourist attraction.

Hastings Pier is a prominent landmark along Hastings's seafront. The old pier was opened in 1872 but was closed in 2006 due to safety concerns from the council. In October 2010 a major fire burned down most of the buildings on the pier and caused further damage to the structure. The pier reopened on 27 April 2016 in a modern architectural form after a £14.2m refurbishment and it won the Stirling Prize of the Royal Institute of British Architects (RIBA) in 2017.

Work on the 910ft pier designed by Eugenius Birch began in December 1869 and it was opened on the first ever August Bank Holiday in 1872. It cost £23,250 and incorporated a 2000-seat pavilion at the seaward end; one of the tollhouses was damaged by a storm in 1877 but was repaired. In 1885 a £2000 landing stage was built and in 1910-11 a small building housing a shooting gallery, 'animated pictures' and slot machines was added, followed in 1912 by a rifle range and bowling alley. This shoreward end of the pier, known as the 'parade extension' was sold to the council in 2013 to finance a new arcade, shops and tea room.

The pavilion was destroyed by fire on 15 July 1917 but was replaced in 1922 in a less elaborate style but it played host in the 1960s and '70s to artists such as The Rolling Stones, The Who, Jimi Hendrix, Genesis, Tom Jones and Pink Floyd; the Pink Floyd founder Syd Barratt playing his last show here with the band on 20 January 1968. A shoreward end pavilion was built in 1926 and an Art Deco façade was added in the 1930s. The pier's seaward end was damaged by storms in

1938, closing the pavilion and costing £22,000 to repair. The pier was sectioned during WWII and was taken over by the armed forces; it suffered some bomb damage during the conflict and reopened in 1946. The West View and East View solaria were added in 1951 and 1956 respectively.

Hastings Pier.

In 1966 Hastings Council built the 'Triodome' on the parade extension to house a special embroidery marking the 900th anniversary of the Battle of Hastings. The extension and Triodome were sold to the pier company in 1968. In 1969 the Triodome was converted into an amusement arcade and the bandstand shelters became kiosks and shops.

In June 2006 following the serving of a closure notice by Hastings Council the pier was closed. In 2007 after repair work had been carried out beneath the former theatre the central section of the pier was reopened in July 2007 only to be temporarily closed again a few weeks later following a storm in which the pier was struck by lightning causing the emergency evacuation of visitors. Little was done to protect and preserve the pier structure and in March 2008 further damage was caused to the seaward end of the pier during strong winds and very rough seas. In the early hours of 5 October 2010, a devastating fire swept through the pier destroying most of the super structure. Two men were arrested on suspicion of arson and bailed pending further action but the case dragged on until in April 2011 the CPS decided not to charge anyone due to lack of evidence.

The pier finally reopened in April 2016 nearly six years after it was almost totally destroyed by the fire. The former pavilion which had now been converted to a restaurant and bar opened to the public and people could stroll around the entire pier for the first time in ten years. On Saturday 21 May 2016 Hastings Pier was officially re-opened. The ceremony included speeches from funders and politicians before celebrations began, finishing with a concert by the pop group Madness.

East Hill Cliff Railway or East Hill Lift is a funicular railway (a form of cable railway which connects points along a railway laid on a steep slope) which provides access to Hastings Country Park via the East Hill which overlooks the Old Town and Rock-a-Nore, an area to the east of Hastings. From here there are views over The Stade (a shingle beach which has been used for beaching boats for over 1000 years) home to the largest beach-launched fishing fleet in Europe. The line is owned and operated by Hastings Borough Council with the following specifications:

Length - 267 feet (81m)
Gradient - 78%
Cars - 2
Capacity – 16 passengers per car
Configuration – Double track
Gauge – 5 ft (1,524 mm)
Traction - Electricity

East Hill Lift.

It was opened in August 1902 by Hastings Borough Council and was originally operated on the water balance principle and the twin towers of the upper station contained water tanks for this purpose. The line was modernised between 1973-76 when it was converted to electric operation and new cars were provided. In June 2007 the line was closed due to an incident where a fault in a control panel caused the cars not to stop at the correct point causing damage to both cars and stations. In 2008 Hastings Borough Council decided on a major refurbishment which involved new cars and new control and safety systems as well as repairs to the damaged stations; the line reopened in March 2010.

After the closure of lines in Broadstairs and Margate the East Cliff Railway became the steepest funicular in the UK. The line is complemented by the West Hill Railway which provides access to Hastings Castle and the Smugglers Adventure in St Clements Caves.

Hastings Country Park (which you will visit on Walk 17) is the most prestigious area of biodiversity management and the largest area of public open space in the borough. The reserve consists of Hastings Cliffs Special Area of Conservation, Hastings Cliffs to Pett Beach Site of Special Scientific Interest and Hastings Country Park as well as heritage designations such as scheduled ancient monument. The area is renowned as an area of archaeological importance and all the various designations and land uses were brought together under the Local Nature Reserve designation in 2006 to provide a focus for future management.

It is an area of ancient gill woodland, maritime cliff and slope, cliff top grassland and mixed heather, lowland meadow and sustainably managed farmland. The reserve covers 853 acres (345 hectares) together with five kilometres of soft rock cliffs and coastline. Some of the best views of the south east coast can be experienced from the cliff tops and on clear days you can see along the coastline from Beachy Head to Dungeness and as far afield as Folkestone and the French coast.

The site is an outstanding area for birdwatching with many species breeding throughout the various habitats. Many rare and scarce liverworts, mosses and lichens occur within the gills. Peregrines, black redstarts and fulmars breed on the cliffs and Dartford warblers, stonechats and yellowhammers breed on the gorse-covered hillsides. Many migrant species pass through in the spring and autumn which include a few rarities such as Sardinian warbler, red-rumped swallow and Pallas's warbler.

A large population of dormice occur within the woodland and stoats and weasels are also regularly seen. Dolphin and porpoise can occasionally be seen offshore from the cliff top watch points. There is an amazing diversity of invertebrates that live in the cliff habitats and within the heathland and acid grassland including some species which occur in very few other places in Britain; these include the hedgehog weevil, the ant mimic ground spider and the nomad bee.

The cliffs are rich in fossils and have yielded many specimens of dinosaur, pterosaurs, turtles, crocodiles and plesiosaurs. The site is also one of only a handful of sites in the world to have produced early mammal fossils.

Hastings Country Park.

Fairlight Radar Tower.

Fairlight Radar Tower is operated by the coastguard to monitor shipping in the English Channel, the coastguard having been active here since the late eighteenth century. The tower is passed on walk 17.

As you can imagine Hastings has many pubs and restaurants to choose from but I am going to highlight one for a reason you may not expect. The Stag Inn at 14 All Saints Street may not be the pub you choose based solely on its façade; however, it is one of the oldest pubs in Hastings and is a feature on the town's guided walks. You may meet one of the ghosts reputed to frequent the pub; a Dutch sea captain murdered by Hastings's fishermen has been seen in the cellar and there have been reports of a young girl dressed all in white by the fireplace on the upper floor. The back bedroom gives guests goosebumps as they sense a presence.

The pub has historical connections with notorious smuggling gangs and characters from folklore. In the cellar there is a now-blocked entrance to a secret passage which led to All Saints' church that was probably used by smugglers in the eighteenth century, or as a bolt-hole during times of religious oppression.

Whether you believe in ghosts or not what you will find interesting are the famous mummified cats that were found in a chimney during the 1940s which are now on display in the front bar. This wasn't uncommon as cats were often used as a form of protection in old buildings and these cats protect the Stag from evil spirits and harm; it is told that they once belonged to Hannah Clarke who was a witch who is said to have occupied the Stag in its early days.

John Logie Baird lived in Hastings in the 1920s where he carried out experiments that led to the transmission of the first television image. Many notable figures were born, raised or lived in Hastings including computer scientist Alan Turing comedian Jo Brand, singer Suggs (Madness) and Gareth Barry who holds the record number of appearances in the Premier League was born here. Harry H. Corbett (Steptoe & Son) lived in Hastings until his death in 1982.

Now you can do the short but very strenuous walk at Hastings Country Park to reach Fairlight Radar Tower. Our next visit is at Fairlight, Pett and historic Winchelsea where we visit Spike Milligan's grave with the famous words 'I told you I was ill' written in Gaelic.

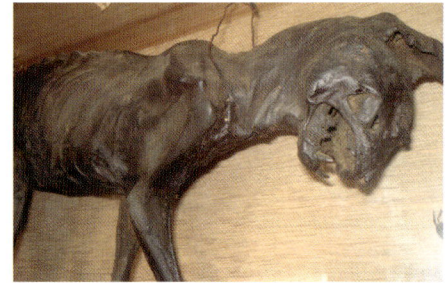

Mummified cats at the Stag Inn, 14 All Saints St.

SUGGESTED WALK

WALK 17. Hastings Country Park & Fairlight Radar Tower. (4.5 miles 7.2 km)

Parking. Barley Lane car park just before the entrance to Shear Barn Holiday Park (Post code TN35 5NT). This 4.5 mile walk really does feel more like a 7mile walk. Between the start and Fairlight Radar Tower it consists of steep climbs and descents and I estimate that there are over 250 steps within the woodland that you have to negotiate but there are no stiles. The Park is well signposted but at the time of writing a couple of the marker posts have lost their numbers as the plates are only stuck on. Refreshments are available from the Coastguards Tea Room by Fairlight Radar Tower.

1. From the car park go through the gate that is to the left of the notice board, opposite the car park entrance. Follow the path down, going down many steps and at a junction go right (not over the bridge) and follow the wide track which curves left and climbs gradually. At the next junction go right and walk with a wire fence on your left. At a junction go left to a viewing bench at Ecclesbourne Glen with cliff views.

View from Ecclesbourne Glen.

Now turn back and walk up the wide grassy path with hedgerow on your right. Climb fairly steeply between blackberry bushes then continue passing to the right of a gate past marker post 8. At a junction by a bench and marker post 12 take the right path signed Firehills 1.5 miles. Follow the path carefully down steps passing marker post 14 and continuing down (not left) and at marker post 16

Steep climbs and descents throughout the walk.

continue down (not left). Cross a stream and climb steeply up the other side. At a bench go left and continue climbing.

At a junction go right at marker post 17 (Firehills 1 mile) and climb steeply again, now climbing steps. Continue then descend more steps with a view of the Fairlight Radar Tower on your left which you will soon be passing (or looking at that hill maybe not so soon). Go through a swing gate and continue down using the right-hand path which is a little uneven.

Pass another marker post (not numbered but Visitors Centre 3/4 mile), then cross a stream and continue climbing steeply again. Climb steps (ignoring the left path) and at the top go right by a marker post (not numbered). At a viewing bench go left through a swing gate to arrive beside Fairlight Radar Tower. (Further along the coast is Fairlight Cove which is described in Chapter 14.)

The views are popular with painters.

2. Go left and follow the wooden perimeter fence around the tower to reach a 3-way footpath sign in sight. (50 yards to the right of the footpath sign is a nice viewing point.) Go ahead up the access road signed as Visitor Centre passing Firehill Cottages on the left and follow the access road passing a car park with nice views beyond it that is popular with painters. Just before the Visitor Centre and Tea Room go left at a 4-way footpath sign and go through a swing gate and along a stony track. Go down steps and at a junction, take care and go down a few awkward stone steps. (You will be pleased to know that from here the rest of the walk is easy and level.)

3. Follow the winding path passing interesting rock formations at Fairlight Sand Quarry, there is an information board here. Just follow the wide path ahead, ignoring any side paths. Pass marker post 20 on your left and continue for a few yards to a 3-way footpath sign. Go left, signed Barley Lane, and go through two swing gates and ahead along a left field edge. Pass marker post 19 on your left and continue ahead. Just keep going until you reach a lane by a 4-way footpath sign. Go ahead along the quiet lane signed to Barley Lane. Pass an artistic sign post on the left saying Hastings 2 miles and continue. When the lane ends continue ahead along the uneven access lane. Soon you reach Shear Barn Holiday Park Reception and 15 yards past it you arrive back at the car park.

Fairlight Sand Quarry.

Artistic sign post.

CHAPTER 14
FAIRLIGHT, PETT & WINCHELSEA

FAIRLIGHT

Fairlight is a village within the Rother District, 3 miles (5 km) to the east of Hastings. The village lies on a minor road between Ore, Pett and Winchelsea and St Andrew's church has a tall tower and beacon turret that can be seen for miles around. Richard D'Oyly Carte who was the founder of the Savoy Theatre, Savoy Hotel and D'Oyly Carte Opera Company which produced the Gilbert and Sullivan light operas is buried in the churchyard.

Fairlight Cove the neighbouring settlement has suffered badly from coastal erosion and landslips by Rockmead Road and Sea Road and a number of properties there are now very close to the sea edge. The Fairlight Preservation Trust, a registered charity, was set up with a view to combating the loss by erosion and more generally to enhance and protect the village. Sea defences were built in the 1990s at Sea Road and in 2007 at Rockmead Road; the 2007 works are intended to be effective for fifty years from that time and are regularly monitored by the Council.

The Hastings Country Park stretches from Hastings to Cliff End on the Pett Levels where it gives access to the beach. This is a favourite spot for fossil hunters; the 'Hastings Beds' are part of the Early Cretaceous Wealden Group aged 140-136 million years.

The highest point in Hastings, now named North's Seat, is at the top of Fairlight Down in the Hastings Country Park, it is named after Frederick North MP who represented the town. He entered Parliament as one of two representatives for Hastings in 1831 and held his seat until 1835 then again between 1854-65 and 1868-69; from this point France can be seen on a clear day. The country park is part of the larger Site of Special Scientific Interest called Hastings Cliffs to Pett Beach. North's Seat can be found by going up Mill Lane to the junction of Fairstone Close (TN35 5EZ) then continue walking up Mill Lane and at the top you reach North's Seat on the left behind hedgerow.

North's Seat.

PETT

Pett is a village located 5 miles (8.0 km) north east of Hastings on the edge of Pett Level, the one-time marshes stretching along the coast of Rye Bay. The road through the village leads down to the second village in the parish Pett Level, the coastal part of which is known as Cliff End. Here there is a beach and as the name suggests, the Weald sandstone cliffs reach their easternmost point. Pett Level is the end for both the Royal Military Canal and the western edge of the 1940s' sea defence wall. The Saxon Shore Way (starts at Gravesend in Kent and traces the coast of south-east England as it was in Roman times to Hastings, 163 miles [262 km] in total) passes through Pett Level.

The manor of Pett belonged to a succession of families including the Halle family, the Levett family, the Fletchers and the Medleys before eventually passing to the Earls of Liverpool.

There is a Site of Special Scientific Interest within the parish, the Hastings Cliffs to Pett Beach which runs along the coast and is of both biological and geological interest. The cliffs hold many fossils and have many habitats including ancient woodland and shingle beaches. The beaches include a sunken forest, a warship that is thought to have sunk in 1690 and at Cliff End the beach contains fossils and dinosaur footprints.

A sunken forest that can be seen in the sand at low tide opposite the Levels is a relic from 8000 years ago when the sea levels were about 100ft (30m) lower than they are today. Melting glaciers have since raised sea levels worldwide and the forest can be seen as spongy wooden roots, fallen trunks and tree stumps across large areas of sand. Sea conditions may bury the remains in sand from time to time until they are uncovered again by storms; the trees have been identified as oak, birch and hazel.

HMS *Anne* was a 70-gun third rate ship of the line of the English Royal Navy, launched in 1678. She was badly damaged at the Battle of Beachy Head on 30 June 1690 and her captain beached her here and set her on fire to prevent capture by the French. Her remains were discovered when the vessel was partly dug up by a mechanical excavator in 1974 and the wreck is usually exposed at low tides. She lies in sand on a firm clay substrate on top of the prehistoric submerged forest and an explanatory panel is placed opposite her location on the sea wall.

Pett Level Beach was the filming location for parts of the video of David Bowie's number one single 'Ashes to Ashes'.

Cliff End from Pett Level East.

WINCHELSEA

Winchelsea is a small town located between the High Weald and Romney Marsh about 2 miles (3.2 km) south west of Rye and 7 miles (11 km) north east of Hastings. The name Winchelsea may be derived from Win from the colloquial word qwent that refers to the marshland behind the town and Chelsea which is rooted in the Saxon word chesil which refers to a shingle beach or embankment. It is claimed by some residents that the town is the smallest town in Britain as there is a mayor and corporation in Winchelsea. The mayor is chosen each year from amongst the members of the corporation, who are known as freemen, rather than elected by public vote; new freemen are themselves chosen by existing members of the corporation. There has been a Mayor of Winchelsea since Edward I granted the town the right to its own mayor and corporation around 1292 and records of the mayors exist since 1295. In its current form the corporation is effectively a relic of Winchelsea's days as a 'rotten borough' (when Winchelsea elected two MPs but the number of voters was restricted to about a dozen, sometimes fewer). The corporation lost its civil and judicial powers in 1886 but was preserved as a charity by an Act of Parliament to maintain the membership of the Cinque Port Confederation. Today the mayor and corporation have a largely ceremonial role, along with the responsibility for ongoing care and maintenance of the main listed monuments in the town and museum.

Old Winchelsea was on a massive shingle bank that protected the confluence of the estuaries of the Rivers, Brede, Rother and Tillingham and provided a sheltered anchorage called the Camber. The old town was recorded as Winceleseia in 1130 and Old Wynchchelse in 1321; the Normans called the place Wincenesel. After the Norman Conquest, Winchelsea was of great importance in cross-channel trade acting in particular as an entrepôt (a port, city or trading post where merchandise may be imported, stored or traded, usually to be exported again) for London and as a naval base. In the thirteenth century it became famous in the wine trade from Gascony in southwestern France.

Today's Winchelsea is the result of the old town's population moving to the present site, when in 1281 King Edward I ordered a planned town, based on a grid layout, to be built. It is recorded that the town planners were Henry le Waleys and Thomas Alard and the new town retained its affiliation to the Cinque Ports Confederation together with Rye and the five head-ports. Winchelsea was greatly involved in the wine trade with Guyenne (another old French province) and the extensive wine cellars, or undercrofts, under the town can be visited on open days. The cellars are an important part of the town's medieval history and visitors can easily identify the tops of cellar entrances at ground level, but the size, scale and beauty of what lies beneath requires a visit down below. Thirty-three accessible cellars exist and the sites of another seventeen are known, they lie mostly in the northern quadrant of the town nearest to the River Brede.

Love, light, peace
Terence Alan (Spike) Milligan c.b.e., k.b.e.
1918 – 2002
Grá mhór ort Shelagh
Writer • Artist • Musician
Humanitarian • Comedian
Dúirt mé leat go mé breoite
Loving father to
Laura • Sean • Silé • Jane
Eternally loved by his grandchildren
Shelagh Margaret Sinclair Milligan
1944 – 2011
Much loved wife, sister & aunt
May they rest together in perpetual light

Spike Milligan's gravestone.

The town had a tidal harbour on the River Brede and flourished until the middle of the fourteenth century; it then suffered French and Spanish raids during the Hundred Years' War until the fifteenth century and it was hit by the Black Death. Camber Castle was built by Henry VIII in the early sixteenth century halfway between Winchelsea and Rye to guard the approach to the Camber; much of the stone used in its construction may have been taken from the demolition of the Franciscan monastery of Greyfriars.

Winchelsea retains its medieval setting on a hill surrounded by largely empty marsh and has many sites of historic interest; the associated walk 18 tries to pass as many of these as possible.

St Thomas the Martyr church dates to the late thirteenth century and was built as part of Edward I's plan for the new town. It stands in a 2-acre site in the centre of the grid pattern established under King Edward's command. The church has an oddly truncated appearance; it is unclear if the original plans for a large cruciform church were never finished or if the absence of a nave, tower and transepts was the result of a French raid in Winchelsea in 1380. Its interior has some of the finest medieval tombs in England, many of them are chantries to the Alard family. The earliest chantry dates to 1312 and features an effigy of Admiral Gervase Alard in armour beneath an ornately carved canopy. Another memorial commemorates archbishop Robert de Winchelsea (b. 1230) who was a native of Winchelsea. More modern highlights include the twentieth century stained-glass windows designed by Douglas Strachan. In the graveyard is the grave of the comedian (Goon) Spike Milligan who had the last laugh when, with agreement with the local diocese over the wording on the headstone of his grave, the epitaph reads: 'I told you I was ill'. Because the local Diocesan authorities thought this to be too light-hearted an inscription to be engraved in English it is written in Gaelic in reference to his Irish ancestry as: 'Dúirt mé leat go raibh mé breoite'.

St Thomas the Martyr.

Effigy of Gervase Alard.

Court Hall is a two-storey medieval building that now houses a museum of local life. It was built in the fourteenth century and has a thirteenth century doorway in the east wall, which was brought from elsewhere. It was used as the Winchelsea Town Hall from 1557 and the Mayor of Winchelsea is elected here annually on Easter Monday; the lower floor was originally used as the town gaol. Museum exhibits include civic regalia, a model of the medieval town, local pottery, paintings, old photographs and civic seals, along with the silver mace used by the town's sergeant-at-arms.

Court Hall and Museum.

Blackfriars Barn.

Blackfriars Barn is the remains of a fourteenth-century building possibly linked to a medieval Dominican friary. Beneath the ruined walls is a fourteenth-century cellar which can sometimes be visited by arrangement with the National Trust and one reason to visit the cellars is to see a series of a dozen ships scratched into the plasterwork. The Dominicans came to Winchelsea in the early fourteenth century but the ruins date from the middle of the fourteenth century. The friary passed into private hands at the Dissolution of the Monasteries and it is likely that stone from the friary was used to build Camber Castle (Camber Castle - see Chapter 14).

New Gate dates to the thirteenth century and straddles Wickham Rock Lane to the southwest of the town. Beside the gateway runs the town ditch which acted as a water channel and secondary line of defence. New Gate failed in its primary defensive purpose as it was through this gateway that the French gained entry to the town in 1380. It is not known for certain but tradition says that a traitor within the walls let them in. The result was devastation; they attacked the town and may have destroyed parts of the church.

New Gate.

Pipewell Gate.

Strand Gate.

Pipewell Gate (Ferry Gate) is the youngest of the three medieval gateways to Winchelsea. The original gate, which gave access to a ferry, was destroyed by the French in the 1380 raid. What is there today is its replacement built in 1404 by the Mayor of Winchelsea, John Helde. The road here plunges downhill beneath a steep cliff and it was here that King Edward I had a miraculous escape. He was at Winchelsea to view the fleet that was being loaded for his Flanders campaign of 1297-8. He approached the top of the cliff, which was crowned only by a low earth wall, when his horse shied. The horse jumped the wall and with its rider disappeared down the precipice. Horror-struck townsfolk were in time to see the horse land a full 30 feet below on the road where it slid twelve paces still with the king in his saddle. The king turned him round with the rein and rode him up to the gate. When he passed through the people standing round were filled with great joy and wonder in contemplation of the divine miracle by which the king was preserved.

Strand Gate is the most impressive medieval gate and it provided access to the port. The impressive gateway dates to the late thirteenth century and has four round towers linked to short sections of wall. The main passage has two portcullises, one at each end. The original tower was one third higher than the tower we see today, with a porter's lodge in the north-eastern tower and a chamber over the central arch for the portcullis winding mechanism. The original gateway would have been rendered white which would have been an impressive sight as you approached from the river.

At the end of Monks Walk you can see a tall gable end of a building linked to a stone wall and this is all that remains of St John's Hospital, an almshouse that catered to the needs of the poor and elderly. Two more almshouses, dedicated to St Bartholomew and the Holy Rood, stood in the field beyond the ruins of St

St John's Hospital ruin.

John Wesley's Chapel.

John's. St John's was the oldest of the three, probably dating to the late thirteenth century. Also in the field are turf-covered foundations of the medieval south suburbs of Winchelsea. This area of the town was abandoned after raids by the French and the slow decline of Winchelsea after its port silted up.

Methodism has a long history in Winchelsea and on Rectory Lane stands the Methodist Chapel built in 1785. John Wesley preached here in 1771 and made such an impression that the townsfolk banded together and erected the chapel, which remains basically unaltered to this day. Wesley returned to preach in the chapel in 1789 and 1790 and on the last occasion, such was the interest in hearing him speak that the chapel was deemed too small, but he was barred from using the parish church. Instead, he spoke in the open air, seated beneath an elm tree almost opposite the New Inn. Unfortunately, Wesley was so popular and so far-reaching his legacy, that 'Wesley's Tree' became a target for souvenir hunters, who damaged the tree so badly that it died. A sapling from the original elm

Wesley's Tree.

The Well House (Town Well).

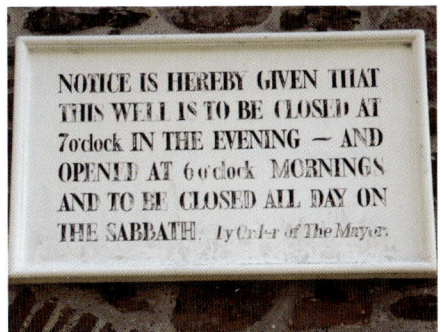 

was planted in its place and this descendant of the original tree thrives. Across from Wesley's Tree is New Inn an eighteenth-century coaching inn.

The Well House (Town Well) is a pyramidal building on Castle Street which houses the town well, a gift to the community by Thomas Dawes who had the well sunk in 1851. The building is Victorian but it reuses medieval arches and buttresses. The shaft below the well preserved well mechanism plunges 130 feet down and is lined with red brick. A notice on the outside reads: 'Notice is hereby given that the well is to be closed at 7 o'clock in the evening and opened at 6 o'clock in the morning and to be closed all day on the Sabbath. By Order of The Mayor'.

There is also a sign which reads: 'Caution. All persons are strictly cautioned against throwing anything whatever down the town well. As the police have orders to report immediately any act of nuisance, so that the offenders may be prosecuted'. Dated the 11th Day of July 1872. By Order of The Magistrates.

The Royal Military Canal (RMC) stretches for 28 miles (45 km) hugging the old cliff line that borders the Romney Marsh from Hythe in the north east to Cliff End in the south west. It was built as a third line of defence against Napoleon, after the British Royal Navy patrolling the English Channel and the line of 74 Martello Towers built along the south coast. The RMC was constructed in two sections: the longest section begins at Hythe in Kent and ends at Iden Lock in East Sussex; the smaller section runs from the foot of Winchelsea Hill to Cliff End. Both sections are linked by the Rivers Rother and Brede.

Royal Military Canal (RMC).

The first cut of the RMC was dug at Seabrook, Kent on 30 October 1804. The canal was completed in April 1809 at a cost of £234,000 (£10m at today's rate). The canal was dug by hand by 'navigators' who were workmen who travelled the country building the canals at the time. The excavated soil was piled up on the landward side to form a parapet to enable troops to move along the canal protected from enemy fire; a narrower road was built on the seaward side as a towpath for the horses pulling the barges. Every 500 metres along the canal's length a kink was made to enable canons to be fired down each stretch.

'Station Houses' were built at every bridge along the canal, these were actually guard houses and one of the roles of the soldiers posted in these houses was to control smuggling which was rife on the Romney Marsh at the time. However, the soldiers were often corrupt and could easily be bribed by the smugglers with either money or contraband goods. Shortly after construction of the canal, Preventative Officers were also employed on the Marsh to catch smugglers; while easy to bribe, the officers were paid according to how many smugglers they caught which was a greater incentive to carry out their duties properly.

After the war, a barge service was established from Hythe to Rye. The government abandoned the canal in 1877 and leased it to the Lords of the Level of Romney Marsh. The canal is now used by the Environment Agency to manage water levels across much of the Marsh and is vital to the areas flood protection.

Now you can do the associated walk to visit as many of Winchelsea's attractions as I could fit in on the circular walk including Spike Milligan's grave. I will see you in the final chapter where we explore historic Rye before finishing at Camber Sands near the Kent border.

FAIRLIGHT, PETT & WINCHELSEA

SUGGESTED WALK

WALK 18. Historic Winchelsea and Royal Military Canal.
(3.5 miles 5.6 km)

Parking. There is roadside parking opposite the New Inn near Court Hall or nearby (Post code TN36 4EN). This is a fairly short walk that is quite easy going. There is a hill towards the end but is gradual and not too steep; there is one stile. Refreshments are available from the New Inn.

1. As you will quickly notice Winchelsea does not have any road names. I will give the names of the roads but will have to describe the turnings. With your back to the pub go ahead down the High Street passing Court Hall & Museum on the left and St Thomas the Martyr church on the right. The church is worth visiting for its artefacts and stained-glass windows. Spike Milligan's grave can be found opposite the church entrance beneath a large tree. Turn first left (after The Little Shop) along Castle Street immediately passing the Well House on the right; remember to look at the signs above the arch. Take the first left (after The Old Post Office) along Mill Road and then the first right (after Manna Plat) along School Hill. At the end you need to go right but a short distance to your left, in view, is Pipewell Gate which is worth the short detour – read what is on the blue plaque regarding King Edward I.

Having turned right take the first right up Castle Street then go left along Mill Road (passing Five Chimneys) and at the end go right (by Alards) along Barrack Square. Take the first left (after The Retreat) and go down Strand Hill passing through Strand Gate. At the end go right down the A259 (Tanyard Lane) using the left-hand pavement.

The New Inn.

Spike Milligan's Grave.

2. At a bend, cross over and go right along the road signposted to Winchelsea Beach. Cross the Royal Military Canal (RMC) and immediately go right and walk with the canal on your right; there is a good view of Strand Gate on top of the hill on your right. Just follow the canal and cross a stile to the left of a wide metal gate. Continue for another 100 yards then go right over a bridge by a 4-way footpath sign. On the other side of the canal go straight ahead aiming for the trees ahead, then follow them to the right for a few yards then left to reach a lane. Go right along the lane (Monks Walk) to reach New Gate which has a blue information sign on it. Continue up the lane, climbing gradually, to reach the ruin of St John's Hospital at the end on the left.

The Well House (Town Well).

Strand Gate from Royal Military Canal.

3. At the end go right along the road, signed to Winchelsea, using the left-hand pavement. Turn left along the road that is opposite the church on your right and at the end go right to reach John Wesley's Chapel on the right with Blackfriars Barn & Cellar directly opposite. Continue along the road and go first right back to the New Inn at the start. John Wesley's Tree is along the road on the right just past the New Inn, it is the first tree on the left.

New Gate.

CHAPTER 15
RYE & CAMBER

RYE

Rye is a small town 2 miles from the sea at the confluence of three rivers: the Rother, Tillingham and Brede. In medieval times, as an important member of the Cinque Ports Confederation, it was at the head of a bay of the English Channel almost entirely surrounded by sea. In days gone by Rye was involved in smuggling and the notorious Hawkhurst Gang, who operated between 1735-49, used its ancient inns The Mermaid Inn and The Olde Bell Inn which are said to be connected to each other by a secret passageway.

Medieval maps show that Rye was originally located on a huge bay of the English Channel called Rye Camber which provided a safe anchorage and harbour. As early as Roman times, Rye was important as a place of shipment and storage of iron from the Wealden iron industry. As one of the two 'Antient Townes', Winchelsea being the other, Rye became a limb of the Cinque Ports Confederation by 1189 and then a full member; protection of the town as a Cinque Port was very important due to the commerce that trading brought. Rye received its charter from King Edward I in 1289 and acquired privileges and tax exemptions in return for ship-service for the crown.

The River Rother originally took an easterly course to flow into the sea near what is now New Romney but violent storms in the thirteenth century cut the town off from the sea, destroyed Old Winchelsea and changed the course of the Rother. In about 1375 the sea and river combined to destroy the eastern part of the town and ships began to use the current area, the Strand, to unload their cargo. Two years later the town was attacked and burnt by the French and it was ordered that the town walls be completed as defence against foreign raiders.

Rye was considered one of the finest Cinque Ports but constant work was required to stop the silting up of the river and the harbour and Acts of Parliament had to be passed to enable the River Rother to be kept navigable. With the coming of bigger ships and larger deep-water ports, Rye's economy began to decline and fishing and smuggling (including owling – the smuggling of sheep or wool) became more important. Imposition of taxes on goods had encouraged smuggling since 1301 and by the end of the seventeenth century smuggling had become widespread throughout Kent and Sussex with wool being the largest commodity. When luxury goods were added, smuggling became a criminal pursuit and groups such as the Hawkhurst Gang turned to murder and were subsequently hanged.

During the 1803-05 Napoleonic invasion threat, Rye, Dover and Chatham were regarded as the three most likely invasion ports and Rye became the western command centre for the Royal Military Canal but the canal was not completed until after the threat had passed.

Rye Castle (Ypres Tower) is a three-storeyed monument built from iron-stained sandstone; it has the iconic square plan with rounded corner towers that was a typical design of the thirteenth century and it is defended by a portcullis on its north side. The exact date for its construction is not known but the town is mentioned as a potential castle site in documents dated 1226 and 1249 – though it is accepted to have been built in the late 1240s and originally called 'Baddings Tower'. Rye played a small but crucial role in the history of Britain as it was involved in both the defence against and trade with France.

In 1430 after numerous high-profile failures to provide protection to the town, the castle was deemed surplus to requirements and was sold to John de Iprys who converted it into a private home, which led to the name Ypres Tower. The Tower remained in private hands until 1494 when it was re-leased to the town and repurposed as a prison. This arrangement was made permanent in 1518 after the Rye Corporation acquired it for use as a dual prison and courthouse complete with a full-time gaoler by 1796. The prison function continued well into the nineteenth century.

After its disuse as a prison, it was used by the town as a morgue. It was badly damaged during a German air raid in 1942 which destroyed the roof of the Ypres Tower. Repair works took place in the 1950s so that by 1954 Rye Castle Museum was able to take over the first and ground floors and added a basement in 1959. The Tower underwent structural work in 1996-7 and had further repairs and alterations in 2005-7.

Rye Castle (Ypres Tower).

Within the museum is the Rye Gibbet Cage which contains the replica remains of John Breads, a local butcher who was executed and hanged in chains for the murder of Allen Grebell (the Deputy Mayor) in St Mary's churchyard in 1742. The murderer's body was exposed in the cage for many years on Gibbet Marsh, the remainder of the bones being removed by animals or piecemeal by superstitious persons in the belief that the drinking of their infusion in water was a cure for rheumatism. The case of John Breads has a unique place in English history as his trial was presided over by the Mayor of Rye – the man that John Breads had actually intended to murder in the churchyard. During the trial Breads said to Lamb: 'I did not mean to kill Mr Grebell. It was you I meant it for and I would murder you now, if I could'. He was found guilty and sentenced to hang.

Replica of John Breads' remains.

St Mary's church is an Anglican parish church that has been a Grade I listed building since 1951 because of its architectural and historical interest; the church is a cruciform building. Its chancel, the crossings, transepts and the nave were built from 1150-1180 with alterations made in the fifteenth century. North and south aisles were added in the late twelfth century and north and south chapels 1220-1250.

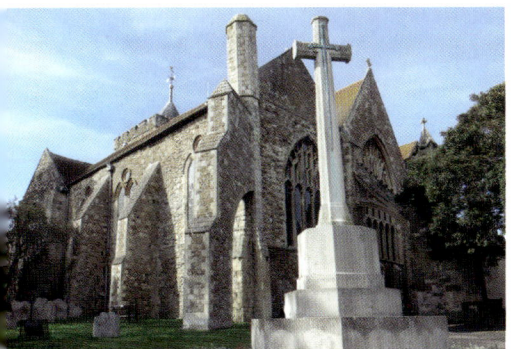

St Mary's church.

Flying buttresses were added at the south east end of the chancel in the fifteenth century and well worked out perpendicular windows can be seen at the east end of the chancel and south chapel. The mayor's seat, which is near the pulpit is from 1547.

St Mary's church has dominated the hill on which the old town stands for more than 900 years. It has the oldest working church tower clock in the country and there are a pair of cherubs perched on the bell tower which were

Top: St Mary's church. Bottom: 'Quarter Boys'.

fitted with complex clockwork mechanisms that allow them to chime the bell at quarter past the hour, hence the name bestowed on them by the town, 'The Quarter Boys'. The new clock was installed around 1561-2 and was made by Huguenot, Lewys Billiard. The pendulum, which is a much later addition, swings in the body of the church. The present exterior clock face and the original 'Quarter Boys' were added in 1760.

St Mary's church bells.

The tower can be climbed to view the clocks workings and for views across Rye and Romney Marsh.

The 'Landgate' is the only surviving fortified entrance to Rye and dates from 1329 in the early years of the reign of King Edward III.

Rye Mill is a Grade II listed building that occupies an historic site in Gibbet's Marsh where a mill has stood in one form or another since at least the sixteenth century; the Symondons map of Rye created in 1594 shows an illustration of a windmill in the exact spot that the mill is today. The first recorded owner of a Rye Mill was Thomas Chatterton who built a 'post mill' in 1758. After his death his widow passed it on to Frederick Barry who demolished it in 1820 to erect a 'smock mill', similar to the one that exists today. Milling continued until 1912 when the premises became a bakery but unluckily on a Friday 13th in 1930 the ovens of the bakery overheated and destroyed the wooden structure on the mill just leaving the two-storey brick base. The mill was rebuilt in 1932 and it continued as a bakery until 1976. The ovens were put to good use when the mill became a pottery and the original oven doors can be seen in the base of the windmill. It became a B&B guesthouse in 1984.

Landgate.

Rye Mill.

Mermaid Street is the most photographed street in the town. The picturesque cobbled street is the location of the Mermaid Inn once used by smugglers and which is reportedly connected by an underground tunnel to The Olde Bell in the High Street for smuggling purposes.

Rye is the location for two Martello Towers. Tower No. 30 is located opposite the turning to Rye Harbour from New Winchelsea Road and it was to protect the sluices of the Brede and Tillingham

Mermaid Inn in Mermaid Street.

rivers. The tower survives well and retains many of its original components and features. The tower was only one of two towers to have been equipped with a cunette (narrow moat in the middle of a dry ditch) at the foot of a slope; the other was at Walton Ferry in Suffolk. The roof retains many of its original features including the inner, and part of the outer, iron gun rails. The tower is privately owned and very difficult to see but it is visited on walk 19; my thanks to the gentleman who allowed me in to take my photo.

Martello Tower No. 28.   Martello Tower No. 30.

Tower No. 28 by the entrance to Rye Harbour was the first tower in Sussex to be built on the west bank of the River Rother and commanded the then entrance to the harbour. It is located in a moat and is known as the 'Enchantress Martello Tower'. The tower survives well and retains many of its original components and features. The upper half of the tower protrudes above the lip of the brick retaining wall of the moat which encircles the base at a distance of around 10 metres and was intended to protect the tower against cannon fire and ground assault.

Rye Harbour is a village near the estuary of the River Rother 2 miles downstream from Rye. The River Rother from Rye seawards and including the village of Rye Harbour is under the control of the Environment Agency. At the village itself there are yacht moorings; a small fishing fleet (coded RX – Rye SusseX); some commercial shipping and a long-established lifeboat station.

Rye Harbour village dates from the early nineteenth century having been built on an extension of the shingle beaches, progressively deposited by the sea over the last 800 years. These deposits limit access to the original medieval port of Rye, which is now 2 miles inland. The village has one of the Martello Towers (No. 28) which was built on the beachline of the time; the beachline has now advanced a further kilometre southward. The initial establishment was that of a company of dragoons in 1805 followed shortly after by the first fisherman's huts and the building of the Martello Tower (1809-10). As the Napoleonic Wars ended the smuggling trade increased in scope and intensity, leading to the establishment of the Coast Blockade. A watch house was built around 1825 to provide shelter and support for the blockade detachments and still stands, complete with the flagstaff for signalling and shipping.

Red-roofed hut and River Rother.

Rye Harbour Nature Reserve was established in 1970 and now receives 360,000 visitors a year. Managed by Sussex Wildlife Trust it has national and international designations and is home to more than 300 rare or endangered species. In May 2021 the Discovery Centre opened on the reserve and contains educational facilities and information about the wildlife; it is a joint project between Sussex Wildlife Trust and the Friends of Rye Harbour Nature Reserve. Look out for the famous red roofed hut, it's in loads of photographs of the reserve.

Within Rye Nature Reserve is the Mary Stanford Lifeboat House. It was built in 1882 and is named after the *Mary Stanford* Lifeboat. On 15 November 1928 the *Mary Stanford* was sadly lost along with all 17 crew; this being the largest loss of life from a single lifeboat in the history of the RNLI and the lifeboat house was never used again.

At 5am the *Mary Stanford* was called to assist a Latvian steamer, the *Alice* of Riga. The crew ran from Rye Harbour to the lifeboat house and launched the boat around 6.45am, in a fierce south-westerly gale. Just as they were leaving, news came that the *Alice's* crew had already been rescued. A signal was fired to recall the *Mary Stanford*, but nobody saw it in the driving rain and the rush to get away. Three and a half hours later, a boy collecting driftwood on Camber Sands saw the *Mary Stanford* capsize; every man on board was drowned. The tightknit fishing community of Rye Harbour was devastated and in the churchyard in Rye Harbour you can see a memorial to the men who served on the *Mary Stanford*. The Lifeboat House and memorial are passed on walk 19.

Camber Castle (known formerly as Winchelsea Castle) is one of a series of forts built by Henry VIII along the south coast to counter the threat of a French invasion during the 1530s. It was built using Wealden and Sussex sandstone and had cost £16,000. Originally the sea came up to the foot of the castle but silting over the centuries means that Camber Castle now stands over a mile from the shore. The castle is typical of Henry's fortresses; a geometric design with rounded bastions arranged around a central tower. The tower was built around 1512 as part of a plan to defend Rye Harbour and the rounded design was intended to deflect cannonballs. It was built by Sir Edward Guildeford who chose a location at the end of a long shingle spit a few metres from the sea. The castle was unaltered for over twenty-five years but a treaty between Spain and France in 1538 put England under threat of an attack by sea. This prompted Henry VIII to begin a programme of strengthening England's coastal defences and that included expanding and strengthening Camber Castle.

In 1539 he had the outer curtain wall built around the tower, which itself was raised in height. Gun platforms were built at alternate corners and a passage was constructed inside the curtain wall, linking the gun platforms. There was originally only a single bastion near the entrance, but c.1542 the castle was altered to a geometric design and the gun platforms were then replaced with four larger bastions fitted out with their own gun ports. The new bastions meant the original ports in the central tower were not required and so the tower was doubled in height. Between the four bastions are stirrup towers which are smaller two-storey D-shaped towers so-named because they resemble a horse stirrup. The bastion and stirrup towers were linked by a mural passage running the entire circumference of the fortifications.

Rye Harbour Nature Reserve.

Within a century the retreating sea meant that the castle was essentially useless; the cannons at the base of the bastions were too low to reach approaching ships so they were raised to roof level but the bastion roofs were too weak for the heavy cannons.

In 1626 Charles I ordered that the castle be destroyed but the order was never carried out. The guns were removed and taken to Rye and for a while the crumbling castle was used as a source of building stone by the locals. The castle sat idle for almost 300 years until in 1943 it was fortified as an anti-aircraft base. After the war it was restored and incorporated into Rye Harbour Nature Reserve with footpaths linking it to Rye Harbour and Rye itself. (It is because it is located within Rye Harbour Nature Reserve that it is described under Rye and not Camber; the castle is passed on walk 19.)

The castle is entered through a gatehouse in the northwest bastion. The central keep is 65 feet across and has 11 ft thick walls; it was originally about half its present height and had 10-gun ports. When Henry VIII strengthened the castle the ground floor was lowered to create a basement and the roof raised to create three floors, you can still see the castle well in the floor of the basement chamber. The west bastion was used as a kitchen and you can still see a large fireplace and double chimneys, as well as a pair of bread ovens built into the fireplace.

The ruins became a popular spot for picnics in the eighteenth and nineteenth centuries and was painted by J.M.W. Turner and plans to develop

Camber Castle.

the castle as a Martello Tower or as a clubhouse for a local golf course came to nothing. The castle is now operated by English Heritage who reopened it, on a very limited basis, to visitors after an extensive programme of conservation between 1968 and 1994; it is an unusual example of an unmodified Device Fort and is a Grade I listed building.

The River Rother flows for 35 miles (56 km) through East Sussex and Kent. Its source is near Rotherfield in East Sussex and its mouth is at Rye Bay, part of the English Channel. Prior to 1287 its mouth was further east at New Romney but it changed its course after a great storm blocked its exit to the sea; until the sixteenth century it was known as Limen. For the last 14 miles (23 km) the river bed is below the high tide level and Scots Float Sluice (at Houghton Green near Playden) is used to control the water levels. It prevents the salt water entering the river system at high tides and retains water in the river during the summer months to ensure the health of the surrounding marsh habitat. Below the sluice the river is tidal for 3.7 miles (6 km).

The River Rother has been used for navigation since Roman times and is still navigable by small boats as far as Bodiam Castle. It became part of a defensive line to protect England from the threat of invasion by the French in the early 1800s when its lower section and part of the River Brede formed a link between the two halves of the Royal Military Canal (described in Chapter 14, Winchelsea).

In 1960 there was extensive flooding of the Rother Valley with 31 square miles (80 km2) inundated and in some areas the water did not recede for several months. In 1962 the Kent River Board introduced a bill to Parliament which would authorise improvements to the river banks, with the construction of a sluice and associated lock below Rye, to prevent tidal flooding. At the time the river was used by a fishing fleet of at least ten trawlers and a 250-ton freighter used the river to trade in timber. However, there was concern in the House of Lords that the lock would not be large enough to accommodate the freighter even though it would be possible to open both sets of lock gates when the tide was suitable. The bill did not become an Act of Parliament due to lack of parliamentary time and so the sluice was not built. The Rother Area Drainage Improvement Scheme did begin in 1966 and was finished in 1980; this involved raising the level of the flood banks along much of the river. The banks in the Wet Level, an area of 690 acres (280 ha) between the junction with the Maytham Sewer and Blackwall Bridge, were not raised as much so that during periods of high flow when the river is tide-locked the levels can be used for storage. The scheme included the installation of 20 pumping stations which raise water from the low-lying marshes into the embanked river using Archimedes' screw pumps. Some of the drainage ditches in the marshland had to be reconfigured to deliver water to the pumping stations.

As you can imaging historic Rye has a large number of bars and restaurants for you to visit and all of them have their own charm and character so like Hastings, I am going to suggest an inn/restaurant/hotel that you may not consider on your visit as it is a four-minute drive outside of Rye.

The Playden Oast Inn is one of the very few oast houses open to the public as most of them have been converted into private properties. The Oast is believed to have been built in 1800; once owned by the Matthews family, it was used as a working oast house to dry locally grown hops for the production of real ale. During its life it has survived two fires, one being on bonfire night in 1970 and the other in the early '80s due to some soldering of copper pipes being done in the attic. The Matthews family sold the Oast in 1971 for just £9000 and today it offers a memorable experience of your day visiting Rye. (The Playden Oast, Rye Road. TN31 7UL.)

The Playden Oast Inn (TN31 7UL).

CAMBER

Camber is a village 3 miles (4.8 km) south east of Rye. The village is located behind the sand dunes that occupy the estuary of the River Rother where the seaside settlement of Camber Sands is located. Camber takes its name from the Camber (la Chambre) the huge embayment of the English Channel located between Rye, Old Winchelsea and Old Romney that was gradually lost to silting-up following changes to the coastline and the changed course of the Eastern River Rother since the Middle Ages.

Camber came into its own with the game of golf. It was originally a collection of fisherman's dwellings but by the early 1890s the number of visitors to Rye increased as tourism became more popular and one result of this was the building in 1894 of Rye Golf Links in the area of sand dunes on the shores of Rye Bay. The Rye and Camber Tramway was a tourist railway opened in 1895 which was originally used for the members of the golf links to carry their gear; it closed to the public at the start of WWII and never reopened. (Camber Castle is described under Rye.)

Camber Sands is a famous beach in the village of Camber. It is the only sand dune system in East Sussex and lies east of the estuary of the River Rother and stretches 3 miles (4.8 km) to just beyond the Kent border where shingle and pebbles return.

A large section of the western end of the dunes lies within the Camber Sands and Rye Saltings Site of Special Scientific Interest (SSSI) while the rest is designated a Site of Nature Conservation Importance. The dunes are getting bigger by accretion (the process of coastal sediment returning to the visible portion of a beach after a submersion event) and they are managed to prevent problems with wind-blown sand. Camber village lies behind the dunes towards the eastern end. East Sussex County Council owns the dunes towards the eastern end which covers about 53 acres and Rye Golf Club owns the western end up to the harbour arm.

Camber Sands looking east towards the Kent border.

Dune systems are formed by a complex interaction between geology, tide, sun, wind and vegetation. Sand is produced by the grinding of the waves or from material brought down by river systems which is deposited along the coast. When the tide goes out (about 1 km at Camber) the sand is dried by the sun and wind and then blown inland by the south-westerly wind; a process called saltation. When the sand meets an obstruction such as vegetation and the wind speeds drop, the sand is deposited and forms dunes. The dunes can be divided into three distinct zones: embryonic fore dunes, unstable yellow dunes running parallel with the coast and stable grey dunes located on the golf course towards the western end of the system.

Camber is an accreting dune system that is gradually getting bigger with 7500 cubic metres of sand deposited here every year. It is part of the Dungeness cuspate foreland, a triangular mass of shingle formed after the last ice age. The dunes have formed over the last 350 years and are now restricted by urban development.

The dunes contain locally and nationally important animal and plant communities. The plants found on the dunes are an important habitat for moths and many scarce species have been recorded here including sand dart, shore waistcoat and white colon. The dunes are also important for wintering birds including hen harrier, short-eared owl, snow bunting, stonechat and sanderling. Habitat types include fore dune, shingle, dune scrub, inter tidal, woodland and acid dune grassland.

In 1939 the coastal land at Camber was used by the War Department for military exercises. Concrete tank traps and pillboxes were built because of the threat of German invasion and the beach was used for practicing beach landing manoeuvres for D-Day. After the war the dunes had to be restored. In 1967 the council carried out major reseeding of the dunes and wind-blown sand was removed to build Dungeness Power Station. In recent years the popularity of Camber Sands has led to a big increase in tourism with up to 25,000 people visiting on hot summer days; this has resulted in further erosion of the dunes.

There are two shipwrecks off the coast of Camber Sands which are partly visible at very low tide. The first and most obvious of the two is the wreck on Broomhill Sands which is that of a fishing trawler. The *Veermann Z300* was built in 1981 and sunk in the English Channel in 1991. An attempt to salvage her in 1992 failed and she re-sank in the position she can now be seen.

Veermann Z300 – Broomfield Sands taken at 1.5m tide.

An older wreck can be seen but only at very low tide near the coast guard cottages at Jurys Gap. HMS *Caulonia* a minesweeper trawler of 296 tons was launched in December 1912 and taken over by the Admiralty in 1942. On 31 March 1943 she ran aground and floundered off Broomhill. Of her 11 crew 7 survived.

Jury's Gap by the seven Coastguard Cottages is effectively on the Kent border with the exception of about a mile of coast which is designated as a 'Danger Area'. The beach is sandy with groynes and when the tide is out it exposes a massive beach. Jury's Gap beach which is also called Broomhill Sands is really the water sports area of Camber Sands and offers excellent conditions for windsurfing and kite surfing. The coastguard cottages are nearly 150 years old and sit on a windswept stretch of countryside between sheep-grazed pastures and the sea. The area here is wilder and more desolate and generations of artists and writers have found inspiration here; the cottages are now let out for quiet creative retreats away from the crowds.

This brings us to the end of the East Sussex coast and the end of my book, once you have done the two associated walks. The famous Camber Sands was an ideal location for me to finish as my West Sussex book basically started with the equally famous West Wittering sandy beach so I have a kind of symmetry across both books. I hope you have enjoyed the book and walks; I can honestly say that I have enjoyed writing it and doing all the walks. The three things I have really taken from this book is visiting the ten Martello Towers as previously I had only passed the one at Seaford and the one at the entrance to Rye Harbour. I was aware of a few more but it was nice to visit all of them to see how they were located to protect the East Sussex coast and how some have since been utilised as either a museum or converted into private residences. The second thing I have discovered is that I want to go back to Herstmonceux Observatory, Seaford Museum and the Brighton Pavilion Museum to appreciate them all properly, I did not have the time on my visits for this book but I do plan to return. The third thing I have learnt is that I still can't spell Herstmonceux right first time, every time – thank goodness for spellcheck. Thanks for buying the book, take care, Phil.

SUGGESTED WALK

WALK 19. Rye Nature Reserve, Camber Castle and two Martello Towers. (8.0 miles 12.9 km).

Parking. Free parking in the large car park at the end of Harbour Road by Martello Tower No. 28 (Post code TN31 7TX). This is a long walk but it is completely level with no stiles. It is best to take your own refreshments.

1. From the car park entrance with Martello Tower No. 28 on your right, go along the concrete access road opposite signed to Rye Harbour Nature Reserve. Go ahead to reach the Discovery Centre in view but take a few looks back as you go to get a nice view of the Martello Tower. Continue past the Discovery Centre as you go heading towards the mouth of the River Rother at the entrance to Rye Harbour. Pass Gooders Hide on the right and the iconic red-roofed hut on the left which seems to be in so many photographs and paintings of Rye Nature Reserve and which had only recently been re-painted ready for my photograph. Continue to the end and just past a pill-box go right along the concrete access road. (Before going right spend a few minutes in this area appreciating the harbour entrance, pill-boxes and views of Camber Sands on the other side of the harbour where you will be walking on the final walk).

Iconic red-roofed hut.   Harbour entrance/River Rother.

Ignore the first footpath to the right and continue past Crittall Hide on the right which offers some lovely views of the birdlife. Ignore the second footpath on the right and pass the Mary Stanford Lifeboat House on the left. (On 15th November 1928, the *Mary Stanford* lifeboat was lost with all 17 crew. This is the largest loss of life from a single lifeboat in the history of the RNLI. This lifeboat house was never used by a lifeboat again. There are information boards here that tell the whole story and we visit the memorial to the 17 crew members at the end of this walk.) Continue past the lifeboat house to reach the next footpath on the right by a 20mph sign and information board for 'Shingle Habitat'.

2. Take this footpath and follow the wide pebble path which soon becomes a narrower undulating path. When you reach a wide gravel access track go 5 yards

Cormorants from Crittall Hide.

Mary Stanford Lifeboat House.

to the right then go left along a wide track with a large lake on your right. Follow the footpath sign directing you to the left of a wide gate and continue ahead. Just past another gate, at a junction, continue ahead along an access track to arrive at a 4-way footpath sign to the left of a stile. Do not cross the stile but go right through a wide gate, signed Camber Cottage and follow the enclosed path. Go through two metal gates and then a wooden gate and continue along a right field edge to reach another gate with views of Camber Castle. (From here there are options of how you can reach the castle but we are going via another lake.)

Go through the gate and turn right to follow the track ignoring any side paths. Soon you will curve to the left and have a wire fence on your right. About 40 yards before a gate in view ahead there is an unmarked path through the trees on your left (opposite it on the right is a number 10 on a fence post). Go left here and immediately pass another lovely lake on the right which may have birds on it. At the end you reach a field with Camber Castle ahead. Make you way over to the castle aiming just to the left of it. (NOTE: as you walk over make a note of the gate that is about 40 yards to the left of it as this is your onward route.) As you approach the castle go over to it and walk anticlockwise around it remembering that originally the sea came up to the foot of the castle but know due to silting it is over a mile from the sea.

3. After walking around the Castle you end up near to the gate that I pointed out to you. Don't go through the gate but you will easily notice a wire fence that goes to the gate and runs right towards Rye. Just turn right and walk with this fence on your left as we now head to Martello Tower No. 30 which is basically in

Lock on River Brede.

Martello Tower No. 30.

Rye. Just follow this fence aiming for Rye, go through a gate to the right of a wide metal gate and cross a stream. Continue ahead along the raised grassy path heading towards a busy road. The path curves right and you just follow it. When you reach a gate continue ahead with the River Brede on your left (don't go right). Soon the path curves away from the river, goes behind a house, then goes left through a gate to reach an access track. Go right along the track to reach a road at the end. Go left over a lock and go to the end of the road to reach the A259. Disappointingly, the last Martello Tower in East Sussex is directly opposite on private grounds and is badly obscured. It is behind the metal gates so your only view is from about 40 yards left along the main road for a limited view back towards it. (When I started to write this book, I was determined to visit all the Martello Towers on the walks. So far, the towers have all been easily viewable but this one is anything but. However, it does show how the ten East Sussex Martello Towers have been repurposed in many different ways.)

4. Return to the A259 junction and re-cross the river and lock. Now using the right-hand pavement just follow Harbour Road all the way back for about 1.5 miles passing industrial units and retail outlets and near the end you reach the church of the Holy Spirit on the right which has the memorial to the 17-lifeboat crew lost on the *Mary Stanford*. Continue along the road to arrive back at the car park.

Memorial to the *Mary Stanford* lifeboat crew at the Church of the Holy Spirit.

TO THE MEMORY
OF THE SEVENTEEN
BRAVE MEN,
THE CREW OF THE
MARY STANFORD LIFEBOAT,
WHO PERISHED IN
A HEAVY GALE WHILE
GALLANTLY RESPONDING
TO THE CALL FOR HELP
FROM THE
S.S. ALICE OF RIGA
ON THE MORNING OF
THE 15th NOVEMBER 1928

WALKING THE EAST SUSSEX COAST – A COMPANION GUIDE

SUGGESTED WALK

WALK 20. Camber Sands. (3.75 miles 6.0 km – option to extend to 5.75 miles 9.3 km)

Parking. There is plenty of parking in the large Camber Central Car Park but this does get full up on sunny weekends and school holidays (Post code TN31 7RH). The walk will take about 1hr 45mins and the optional detour about 1 hour. This walk is level with one minor climb up through the sand dunes near the end; there are no stiles. Refreshments are available from the cafés at the start/end.

1. From Camber Central Car Park go right along the beach with the sand dunes on your right heading for the mouth of the River Rother in view ahead. As you near the river you will spot the famous red-roofed hut that you passed on walk 19 at Rye Nature Reserve ahead. When you reach the river (keep children away from the edge as there is no barrier to stop them falling) turn right and walk with the River Rother on your left and Rye Golf Club on your right. As you go you will pass the Discovery Centre at Rye Nature Reserve and you also get a good view of Martello Tower No. 28 both on the other side of the river.

2. When you reach the Harbour Master Station go right as directed and follow the perimeter around the station. Go through a small parking area and immediately go right through a metal swing gate; look out for the remains of the old tramlines in this area. Follow the grassy path ahead across Rye Golf Course aiming for the left of the Club House and being mindful of golf balls. Go down the access drive to reach a road. Cross over the road and go right for 5 yards then go left beside a building and go ahead to cross a wooden bridge. On the other side of the bridge go right along a path with Little Cheyne Court wind farm away to your left. At the end of the path, you arrive back at the road and you go left and follow the cycle path past two nice lakes on your left.

River Rother towards Harbour Master Station.

3. Just after the second lake at the end of this path, cross over the main road and go ahead up the right-hand side of a field (it is next to the power pole and this is Camber Western Car Park which is used during the summer season). In the top right-hand corner

Martello Tower No. 28 across the river.

View from sand dunes.

Little Cheyne Court wind farm.

go ahead along the path that is to the right of the parking meter. Now for what you have all been secretly waiting for, climb quite steeply up and over the sand dunes to arrive back on the beach. Turn left back to the start.

4. To extend this walk by about a mile each way you can walk along the seafront path, or beach depending on the tide, and walk along to the Coastguard Cottages at Jury's Gap by the Kent border. If the tide is out, you will see the wreck of the Veermann Z300 just before Jury's Gap and Dungeness Nuclear Power Station ahead of you in Kent which is in the process of being decommissioned. As you walk along you will see the large rocks stacked up by the sea wall and the tide comes in very quickly up to the rocks also submerging the lower access steps.

Coastguard Cottages at Jury's Gap.

Steps are partly submerged at high tide.

WEBLIOGRAPHY

www.brighton-hove.gov.uk/chattri-memorial
www.volksrailway.org.uk
www.mybrightonandhove.org.uk/seafront-attractions
www.roedean.co.uk
www.brightonmarina.co.uk
www.thegreenwichmeridian.org
www.eastsussexww1.org.uk
www.newhavenfort.org.uk
www.visitsoutheastengland.com
www.thekeep.info
www.geograph.org
www.eastbourneherald.co.uk
www.seafordmuseum.co.uk
www.things-to-do-in-sussex.co.uk
www.teaantiques.com
www.sussexlive.co.uk
www.orig.villagenet.co.uk
www.trinityhouse.co.uk
www.orchardmemorials.co.uk
www.historicengland.org.uk
www.dnw.co.uk
www.eastbournebandstand.co.uk
www.eastbournepier.com
www.visiteastbourne.com
www.eastbourne redoubt.co.uk
www.castles.nl
www.herstmonceuxparish.org.uk
www.sgf.rgo.ac.uk
www.windmillhill.org
www.herstmonceuxandwartlingchurches.com
www.eastbourneguide.com
www.dolomedes.org.uk
www.guitarhaven.co.uk/minthouse
www.odddaysout.co.uk
www.martellotowers.co.uk
www.thestarinnnormansbay.co.uk
www.visit1066country.com
www.piers.org.uk
www.hastings.gov.uk
www.staghastings.co.uk
www.britainexpress.com
www.winchelsea.com
www.eastsussex.gov.uk
www.eastsussex.gov.uk
www.castrumtocastle.com
www.ryenews.org.uk
www.ryewindmill.co.uk
www.camberhistory.co.uk

ADDITIONAL SOURCES OF INFORMATION

Information boards at numerous attractions and places of interest.
Domesday Book – Penguin Classics 'A Complete Translation' ISBN 0-141-43994-7
All photos taken by Phil Christian.

SELECTIVE INDEX

Beachy Head 74
Bexhill 104
Birling Gap 71
Bodiam 112
Brighton 7
Camber 152
Cuckmere Haven 63
East Dean 70
Eastbourne 79
English Channel 35
Exceat 62
Fairlight 129
Hastings 120
Herstmonceux 90
Hove 8
Jury's Gap 154
Litlington 53

Newhaven 30
Normans Bay 103
Peacehaven 25
Pett 130
Pevensey 97
Piddinghoe 34
Rottingdean 15
Rye 141
Saltdean 18
Seaford 45
St. Leonards-on-Sea 118
Telscombe 24
The Seven Sisters 64
Tide Mills 44
Wilmington 55
Winchelsea 131